Cameos of the Western Front

In the Shadow of Hell

Behind the lines in Poperinghe

Cameos of the Western Front

In the Shadow of Hell

Behind the lines in Poperinghe

by Paul Chapman

Edited by
Ted Smith

with an introduction by
Mary Ellen Freeman

LEO COOPER

By the same group of authors in the Cameos of the Western Front series:

The Anatomy of a Raid
Australians at Celtic Wood, October 9th, 1917

Salient Points One
Ypres Sector 1914 - 1918

Salient Points Two
Ypres Sector 1914 - 1918

Salient Points Three
Ypres Sector 1914 - 1918

A Walk Round Plugstreet
Ypres Sector 1914 - 1918

Poets & Pals of Picardy
A Weekend on the Somme with Mary Ellen Freeman

A Haven in Hell
Ypres Sector 1914 - 1918

First Published in 2001 by
Leo Cooper/an imprint of Pen & Sword Books Limited
47 Church Street
Barnsley
South Yorkshire S70 2AS

Front cover design by Ted Smith from an idea by Jim Ludden

A CIP catalogue record for this book is available
from the British Library
ISBN 0 85052 809 7

Typeset by IMCC Ltd. in 10 point Garamond
Printed in Great Britain by

CONTENTS

Page

DEDICATION

To Bertha Tally and the people of Poperinghe.

ACKNOWLEDGMENTS

To Sandra and Angela

When the original manuscript of *A Haven In Hell* was submitted for publication the decision was made to edit out much of the peripheral information contained therein, concentrating solely on that specifically relating to Talbot House. It is my hope that this book, the story of Poperinghe and its role in the Great War from both the soldier and civilian point, having had its beginnings in *A Haven In Hell*, will prove a worthy companion to that work.

I acknowledge unreservedly that this book owes much to the enthusiastic support, encouragement, and assistance of my friends, Ted Smith and Tony Spagnoly, to whom I owe an eternal debt of gratitude.

I am also particularly indebted to Mary Ellen Freeman for writing the Introduction to this book, and to my friend and mentor, Gladys Lunn and to Jacques Ryckebosch for his support, assistance with research and, despite his busy workload, always finding time to answer many queries.

To the staff of the Commonwealth War Graves Commission, Maidenhead and Ypres, for their assistance and permission to quote verbatim the details of the cemeteries and fallen contained herein. Thanks also to Major Tonie and Valmai Holt, Ann Clayton for her support and permission to quote from 'Chavasse, Double VC' and 'Martin-Leake, Double VC', Major Lake, Royal Welch Fusiliers, for 'The War The Infantry Knew' and a special thank you to Lyn Macdonald for her kind encouragement, advice and permission to quote from some of her many books. And to Wendy Attreed for taking time out from her studies to search the Internet for me.

I am also grateful to Peter Attreed, Peter Barton (Parapet Productions/Foxy Films), Lance Corporal Stuart Bingley, RHQ. Coldstream Guards, Mark Hemsley, Brian Little, Ruth Prince, Jeanne Battheu, Gino and Rita Clabau, Christiaan DePoorter, Jan Louagie, George Sutherland, and Filip and Leila VanSpranghe. And finally a big 'Thank You!' to my publishers Pen & Sword Bools Ltd. for having faith in me.

At the time of going to press the literary executors of certain authors have not been traced and the author will be grateful for any information as to their identity and whereabouts.

Paul Chapman March 2001

INTRODUCTION

Although we look to the Great War from a very different world to that which first saw the names and associated images of the Ypres Salient secure such prominence in our nation's consciousness, human nature has, across a century's divide, remained essentially unchanged. From within an historical and cultural time-frame, the experiences of the men who fought in the Great War provide a touchstone by which we may gain insight into the complexities of the human condition and so, consequently, further an increased understanding of ourselves as fellow mortals. The validity of these men's lives is therefore as relevant to us today as it will prove to future generations – such is the enduring importance of this remarkable epoch of mankind.

I myself, come from a generation where, those of us lucky enough to have grandfathers who returned safely from this war, can remember childhoods interlaced with snippets of overheard adult conversations about things that, although we didn't fully comprehend, we nonetheless were intrigued by in our instinctive awareness of importance. Amongst others, names such as Thiepval, Passchendaele and Wipers, which took seed in my imagination as fragments of a mysterious world exclusive to those who had shared in it and which we on the outside would never fully be able to penetrate. Charles Carrington reflects this perfectly when he described himself and fellow Great War veterans, such as my Grandfather, as "... an initiate generation, possessing a secret that can never be communicated." Nevertheless, our drive to understand their world and their experience within it is arguably intensifying as the years elapse and, fundamental to this understanding, is the need for us to attempt to review every possible facet of that experience in order to give these men their long overdue 'due'!

Each year a profusion of books are published on a variety of subjects within the scope of this war. Many are to be seen tucked under the arms of pensive battlefield visitors as they seek out those landmarks of war amongst the emotively familiar names of the old salient: Bus House, Hill 60, Larch Wood – to name but a few. *In the Shadow of Hell* adds an entirely new perspective by centring on Poperinghe and its surrounding lesser-known places of the salient; places which extend the hidden subculture of this little area of Belgium. Paul Chapman's well-chosen title consummately reflects the subject matter of his book encompassing as it does, back areas frequented by the men, billets and rest camps where they lived and places of leisure not usually to be found on battlefield tours. Its chapters will leave the reader with a desire to come off the well-trodden paths of the salient and invest quality time in discovering those places which, so far, have been almost overlooked in their relevance and importance on the established tour routes. How refreshing to discover a fresh area of interest on this war!

Paul's obvious dedication and commitment to thorough research of his subject, together with his extensive Ypres contacts and knowledge of the area, will further reward the reader with a collection of valuable information either difficult to find elsewhere or unique to Paul. Nowhere is this more evident than amongst some fascinating vignettes relating to the cemeteries covered in the latter half of the book: a section that I eagerly consumed, for these are the truly personal stories and histories of the men themselves – surely the single most important factor regarding this war. After reading this book I will want, for example, to visit the 101 men buried in Lijssenthoek Military Cemetery having died from the effects of gas that Paul mentions and I am quite certain that likewise there will be something new for everyone to add to their list of 'must do' on their next battlefield trip.

In an article published in 1711 in The Spectator, Joseph Addison described books as 'legacies to mankind... delivered down from generation to generation as presents to the posterity of those who are as yet unborn.' Having vouchsafed to all those who read its pages a flavour of Poperinghe and the former khaki-clad armies who passed through its portals, Paul Chapman has ensured that *In the Shadow of Hell* will be regarded as a worthy such legacy for posterity.

M. E. Freeman March 2001

EDITOR'S NOTE

The predominance of available research material on the subject of the Great War is written by officers or historians. War diaries, reference volumes, regimental archives and histories, by their very nature, must be so. The other ranks' contributions to information is left to books, memoirs, diaries, the odd article in newspapers and magazines, and their involvement with such works as Hammerton's *I Was There*, and this is not discounting the excellent work of such writers as Frank Richards, Allan Jobson, W. V. Tilsey, Frank Durham, W. R. Kingham, Frank Hawkins, and a host of others.

Whereas this does not affect research on battles, troop movements and their results, it leaves much to be desired when, as with this book, the second in Paul Chapman's trilogy, the information required is less of a chronology of facts and figures, but more an expression of the moods, feelings and experiences of men, out of the line.

In this area, the officer-weighted literature tends to over-state the qualities of some officers, while being a little patronising to those qualities to be found with men of the other ranks – understandable in that they are not likely to criticise their peers, and were hardly likely to get to know the men well – there were too many of them to start with, and why should they anyway? 'The men loved and admired him and would have followed him anywhere', and similar quotations often appearing in regimental histories and biographies, beg the question: did anyone ask the men if they loved or admired this particular officer? – and what would have happened to them if they had not 'followed him anywhere'?

This literature also, unwittingly, emphasises the privileges enjoyed by officers, against the lower expectations of other ranks, whether in the line, during so-called rest periods or for those who were never anywhere near the front line. In the back areas, officers hunted, fished, enjoyed horse-riding outings and events, socialised and moved about the countryside fairly much as they liked. After cleaning-up, de-lousing, re-training, parading for this or that reason, acting as trench diggers, fetching and carrying parties, road-building gangs and a general source of labour, the infantry enjoyed sports' days, football matches, boxing tournaments and concert parties organised for them, but, obviously, were not allowed the freedom they would have liked. When time was allocated for enjoying themselves otherwise, they would visit bars and estaminets for cheap beer and omelettes, or fried eggs, and 'frites de pommes de terre', whilst the officers could visit officers-only establishments and restaurants, and enjoy the finest of foods and good wine whenever they so wished. Then, of course, there were the red and blue light districts. Much can be found on the control and results of the other ranks' visits to the red, but little is to be found of the officers' visits to the blue.

Many officers were aware of the privileges they enjoyed over their troops and made effort to do something about it. Colonel M. C. Clayton of the Cambridgeshires, when addressing the problem of transporting his men from the camp to the town, made it quite clear that Staff should be more sympathetic, with his: *"... greater facilities should have been afforded them (the infantry) for transport. I know that there were many obstacles in the way, but they should, and could, have been overcome."*

What is not so apparent are the 'privileges by default' which Corps men, officers and other ranks alike, enjoyed over their counterparts in the infantry. Life in the line – 3 to 4 days each in the front, support and reserve trenches, – was incomparable with the corresponding days spent by the Town Major's staff, Railway Operating Department troops, Service Corps dump personnel, hospital orderlies, boot-makers, cooks, map-makers, labour gangs, divisional and brigade headquarter staff, and the mass of other personnel so necessary to keep an army at war.

Occasionally, disgruntlement is recorded, as with Captain W. H. L. Watson's: *"Infantry officers walk miles into Poperinghe for their tea and then find the room crowded with those young subalterns who supply us with our bully"*. A reasonably polite comment, but how did a bunch of 'just-out-of-the-line' infantrymen, sitting down for their egg and chips in an estaminet, react to the group of pay clerks sitting at the table alongside? Very little is written on this subject, or on brawls, vandalism, drunkenness or 'crime' in general.

The battalion 'glass house' and 'jankers' were part of the soldier's life, but, in the Poperinghe area as a whole, it was the Area Provost Marshal's job, working with his civilian counterparts, to maintain law and order. In Poperinghe itself, reporting to the APM, it was the Town Major's job to keep the peace.

The third book in this trilogy will document what crime and punishment was all about in this back area, and will give a fair hearing to officers and men, Corps and Regimental, as well as the 'civvy' population.

Ted Smith March 2001

Kaiser Wilhelm II reviewing his field artillery

I look upon the people and the Nation handed on to me as a responsibility conferred upon me by God, and I believe it is written in the Bible that it is my duty to increase this heritage, which one day I shall be called upon to give an account. Whoever tries to interfere with my task I shall crush.

Kaiser William II

1

IN THE BEGINNING

FLANDERS HAS ALWAYS been a popular place for Britain to settle its differences with other European powers and, in August 1914, it was about to do it again, thanks to the aspirations of Kaiser William II who had decided to declare war on France. Belgium suddenly found itself in the path of the Imperial German Army, then on its way to invade and occupy France. In order to secure a quick and decisive victory in the west, Germany had implemented its long-established Schlieffen Plan, the success of which depended heavily on a rapid advance through Artois and Picardy, encircling Paris from the west, to drive the French against two armies deployed against Alsace-Lorraine in the south. To ensure this success meant crossing Belgium – a neutral country. King Albert I of Belgium, having foreseen this threat, requested that France deploy her troops to protect his neutrality. The French General Staff, not contemplating an attack from their north, dismissed the request.

By 5 o'clock on the afternoon of 1 August 1914, a notice headed *Armée de Terre et Armée de Mer. Ordre de Mobilisation Général* had been posted in every city, town and village of France; it was to come into effect the following day. Germany, having declared war on Russia, had turned its attention on her ally France. When, not surprisingly, the German army crossed the border into Belgium near Liege on 4 August, the Belgian King issued the following emotive Order of the Day:

Remember, men of Flanders, the Battle of the Golden Spurs, and you Walloons of Liege, who now hold the place of honour, remember the six hundred Franchimontois.

Nevertheless, by 13 August, Liège had fallen; King Albert then surrendered Brussels, rather than see the capital destroyed, and withdrew his army to Antwerp. Taking advantage of the absence of any opposing troops, and in accordance with its 1914 Army Training Manual, German High Command had ordered the high ground of the Westhoek in Belgian Flanders, be scouted by cavalry units for tactical purposes:

By clearing the terrain the defender must attempt to find a good position for himself, one which offers a wide and uncluttered field of fire. If time permits, this position will be reinforced by means of trenches and fortifications, etc. As appropriate, obstacles will be placed ahead of the front line. So far as is possible, efforts will always be made to take advantage of the lie of the land, dykes, ditches, sunken roads, high ground, etc. The length of the trenches will depend on the time allowed by the enemy.

Poperinghe, within 50-miles of the Calais and Dunkirk Channel ports, and a short distance from the Franco-Belgian border, was a prominent town in the Westhoek and, on 12 September, its Burgomaster issued a proclamation instructing its citizens to remain calm and behave in a non-provocative manner should they encounter German soldiers.

On 4 October the German 3rd Cavalry Brigade, reconnaissance unit of the German 36th Division (Uhlans), arrived in the town. These troops were reputed to be responsible for all manner of atrocities on their way through Belgium but, during their short stay in Poperinghe, apart from breaking a few windows, their behaviour was considered fairly acceptable. After eleven days they left the town, although not without first helping themselves to numerous 'souvenirs' and a large quantity of supplies.

They moved across the nearby French border in the direction of Hazebrouck and the Mont des Cats where they later came into contact with, and were routed by, the British 2nd Cavalry Division who, three days previously, had engaged and heavily defeated the German 4th Cavalry, in southern Belgium, just beyond Messines.

German troops on their way through captured Brussels

A deciding factor in the their departure was the approach of the French 87th and 89th Territorial Divisions commanded by General Bidon. Setting up Staff Headquarters in the town hall, he sent his 87th Division to Ypres and deployed the 89th in a line between Vlamertinghe and Reninghelst. By end November, Poperinghe had become a French Army garrison town.

Meanwhile, much of the town's population chose to become refugees. Women with very young children moved across the nearby border into France, whilst many of the older children, particularly the girls, were evacuated to school colonies in Switzerland. One of these, Bertha Tally, noted:

> I was sent to live in Switzerland with my sister, Angele, and brother, Guillaume; my eldest brother Charlie had to stay behind to help around the house. We were away for just over four years and when we came home we adapted to things very easily, at least Angele and I did. You see, when Guillaume went away he was very young and didn't speak much, when he came back he was fluent in French; our language was Flemish! My father spoke only Flemish, my mother also and the little pidgin English she had learnt from the soldiers who visited our house. My poor parents could not understand a word Guillaume said, for a number of years Angele and I had to act as interpreters between our little brother and our parents - what fun we had!

Achiel van Walleghem, then the Padré of Dickebusch, a village just southeast of Poperinghe, noted in his diary for 30 May 1915:

> At High Mass I announced that the Belgian Government had opened schools in France. Free board and teaching by Belgian schoolmasters and mistresses. I still didn't dare recommend it too much, as I didn't have any details. It was for girls from 8 to 16 and boys from 8 to 14. There was also a poster for farmers which said: 1) Farms were provisionally for rent in France for the duration of the war; 2) There were fields at 150 Fr and 170 Fr a hectare in Calvados; 3) Transport was free from Abeele.

From late May onwards, a great many farmers and their families, with Franco-Belgian government assistance, left Poperinghe and the Westhoek via special trains from nearby Abeele railway station. The trains took them to Normandy and southern France where they worked the farms of the men who had been called-up for service in the French Army. After the war, when the French soldiers returned to civilian life, many of the Belgian farmers stayed on to make their life in France, while those who returned to Belgium had to start anew in what was left of their destroyed homesteads.

This movement of people away from the area was offset by the arrival of refugees from those villages and towns that were now part of the front line, and by incoming British military personnel. By December 1914, British troops had become a common sight in Poperinghe as they passed through the town on their way eastwards to the Ypres Salient. On 1 February 1915, the French Army vacated the town and handed it over to the British when the V Corps, 6th Division, under General Sir Hubert Plumer moved in.

From this date onwards Poperinghe was, as with Veurne 20 miles to the northwest, to remain the only free Belgian town behind the front line. When the war began the town's population numbered 11,790. When the British arrived, it was only 1,115. Within a few months it was 10,967 of which 2,847 were refugees from villages near the front line. The majority of the male population that were eligible for service had already joined the army, the rest awaited conscription. Poperinghe became a town inhabited by the middle-aged, the elderly, an ever growing influx of refugees, and the British Army.

By April 1915 the number of British troops had swollen enormously, the refugees numbered almost 8,000 whilst the count of Poperinghe citizens had fallen to less than 500. By mid-1915, the Ypres–Poperinghe road saw a non-stop flow of refugees from Ypres and its neighbouring villages who had decided to leave, moving westwards. Most walked, carrying what they could of their personal belongings in bundles on their backs, in wheel-barrows, dog-carts, prams, hand-carts and whatever else would transport their worldly goods. Some continued their journey from Poperinghe to villages further away from the front line, but many stayed put. The town housed those who stayed in barns, sheds, outhouses, any empty houses its

Refugees on the move away from their battered villages

authorities were able to commission, and in whatever liveable space that was left available. There then developed a suburbia of shacks constructed from all sorts of materials, not only for housing, but also as premises for the opening of 'shops' run by these 'refugees within their own country'.

Trooper R. A. Lloyd came across a refugee 'dwelling' when moving to a farm billet with the 1st Life Guards. In his book *A Trooper in the Tins*, he describes:

> What a farm it was! A dwelling-house full of refugees about 50 men and women of all ages. I opened a door off the living room and looked into the next apartment. Fully thirty men and women slept any old how on the floor. There was a good fire in the living room and a pump which produced a brown "water" supply, though the surrounding fields were nearly all flooded. The farmyard was one large cesspool, the outbuildings foul... we slept in some hay in the loft over the dwelling-house, just as we were, booted, spurred, and mud-caked, but realising we were in the Carlton compared with our comrades in the front line.
>
> Next morning we were up and astir early. The farm precincts fairly stank. The refugees disappeared about their daily vocations in Poperinghe, and we waded out through the mud to find and tend our horses.

So Poperinghe, differently populated, took on a new rôle behind the Allied front line, a soldier's town – and a place of refuge, in-transit and permanent, for Belgians moving out of their villages within the Ypres Salient.

Part of Poperinghe's new suburbia of shacks

Civilian 'traders' visiting a farm billet

26/8/15. Colonel Trembloy of the Belgian Gendarmerie states that inhabitants of Pop do not consider it fair to billet troops in the town and he shares their belief, that this is the main cause of the bombardments.
Captain E, A. Collins, Town Major, Poperinghe 1915 -1918

2

SOLDIERS & CIVVIES

AFTER FIRST YPRES denied the German Army access to the Channel Ports, the opposing forces dug-in, with both sides facing each other in a 700 kilometre line of trenches from the Belgian coast to the Swiss frontier. This stalemate would not change significantly for the next four years despite intense fighting, terrible destruction, and enormous casualties on both sides. On 4 February 1915, Poperinghe, now strategically the first place of any importance behind the lines in Belgium, was officially declared part of the British sector.

In November 1915, Senior Army Padré Neville Talbot, was instructed to find a house in Poperinghe that could be used as a rest and recreation centre, an alternative to the many bars, cafés and estaminets in the town. By the end of the month he had secured the premises of a local financier. Talbot entrusted the running of this house to fellow padré Philip Clayton. After the destruction of the original Church House, the newly acquired house was to be named similarly but, at the insistence of the Town Major, it was called Talbot House after Neville Talbot, and dedicated by him to the memory of his younger brother Gilbert, who was killed at Hooge on 30 July 1915. Although run by Church of England padrés, Talbot House was non-denominational, offering the same welcome and services to all. Officially opened on 11 December 1915, it remained open throughout the war, apart from a short spell during the summer of 1918.

Destined to become the town's most famous war-time inhabitant, Philip Clayton, better known as 'Tubby' Clayton, co-founder of the house, wrote:

Poperinghe was without a rival locally. Alone free for years among Belgian towns, close enough to the line to be directly accessible to the principal sufferers, and not so near as to be positively ruinous, it became metropolitan not by merit but by logic of locality... Until the great switch road was opened and every mule (whether on four legs or closely packed in a blue 'bully beef' tin) came up by one set of rails or one narrow street.

Designated a British garrison town, Poperinghe became not only a funnel through which British divisions would pass on their way to the front, but also a place where troops could spend some of their spare time. This 'spare time' had its drawbacks for the soldier: there were duties to be performed; personal hygiene to be observed; latrine digging; bayonet practice; tactical practice; route marches; cleaning; tidying, and fetching-and-carrying details. 'Spare time' or 'rest', as it was described by Captain John Milne in *Footprints of the 1/4th Leicestershire Regiment, August 1914 to November 1918,* the regiment's history, reads:

> The phrase "six days' rest" was really a snare and a delusion. In the imagination one looked forward to sleep unlimited, parcels from home galore; letters from at least half-a-dozen armfuls of delicious womanhood alluding affectionately to the joys of past and future "leaves." One had visions of binges in Bailleul, razzles in Reninghelst, and perchance passion in Poperinghe. But in reality "six days' rest" was an entirely different affair. Certainly it began with parcels and sleep, followed by baths and clean clothes, but after that it was sadly tarnished by "The C.O. will inspect," "The battalion will parade," or "A Working Party will be furnished," which meant that companies had to pull themselves together and remember that they were soldiers once more and not semitroglodytes living in trenches and dugouts. And that as soldiers they had to stand smartly to "attention," to "fix bayonets," to keep the thumb in line with the seam of the trousers, and the feet at an angle of forty-five degrees. And, after the morning had been energetically spent in drill and bayonet fighting, they would be gratified to hear that there would be a route march in the afternoon.

The infantry breaking rock for road-building, one of its many 'spare time' activities

When the British took over the town, English became the third language spoken by the inhabitants, after Flemish and French - the British Army issued simple phrase books to the soldiers, resulting in a fourth and fifth language coming into being – Flemglish and Franglais!

Captain J. C. Dunn, Medical Officer of the 2nd Battalion Royal Welch Fusiliers, wrote:

> The people hereabout are Flemish in appearance, and bi-lingual; a few speak Flemish only. Dull Flemings they are not, but a talkative lively people, more so than those of any part I have been in yet. They spoke Flemish among themselves, not French. To requests for cigarettes or matches from the men they replied, "N'y a pus," the local dialect for "Il n'y en a plus," from which "na'poo," soon an expressive word in the Army's daily speech evolved.

Many regulars of the British Expeditionary Force had seen service on the Northwest Frontier of India, and were of the opinion that all foreigners would understand the language the British used there. On arriving in France, Private Frank Richards, also of the 2nd Battalion Royal Welch Fusiliers, writes in his book, *Old Soldiers Never Die*:

> Billy used to boast that no matter what new country he went to he could always make the natives understand what he required. He ordered a bottle of red wine, speaking in English, Hindustani and Chinese, with one word of French to help him out. The landlord did not understand him and Billy cursed him in good Hindustani and told him he did not understand his own language, threatening to knock hell out of him if he did not hurry up with the wine. One of our chaps, who spoke a little French, told the landlord what Billy required. The wine was brought. I remonstrated with Billy and told him we could not treat the French, who were our allies, the same as we treated the eastern races. He said: 'Look here, Dick, there is only one way to treat foreigners from Hong Kong to France, and that is to knock hell out of them'.

The majority of these regulars had, at best, received a basic education. Officers came mostly from the upper echelons of society and had at least some knowledge of foreign languages – normally French and Latin. It was small wonder that many of the men, being unable to grasp the pronunciation of French and Flemish names, used easier-to-understand alternatives; Dickebusch became *Dickiebush*, Ypres – *Wipers* (reputed to have been first used in this form by Sir John French), Wytschaete – *Whitesheet*, Ploegsteert – *Plugstreet*, Godewaersvelde – *God-wears-velvet*, while Poperinghe became affectionately known as *Pop* or *Pops*.

Of the towns and villages in the back areas, Poperinghe was the most popular with the troops. Popularly referred-to as the 'Capital' of the Salient, as an officer of the 1st/2nd London Regiment was to remember:

Pop to the British Army was best known and most frequented. Here there was Skindles and Cyrilles' restaurants always full of officers of every Corps, enjoying the excellent meals provided. Here, too, was the original Toc H, the seed from which was to spring a now world-wide organisation of brotherhood; the officers' club, through whose roof the shells of a German long-range gun came one morning in 1917 killing several officers on their way home from leave; the station within easy range of the bigger guns, whence leave-trains daily departed, and where, despite alterations in the times of departure, the enemy would make direct hits on departing trains with distressing frequency.

Private Allan Tobson of the Royal Army Medical Corps, serving with the 39th Divisional Field Ambulances, was to say in his book, *via Ypres*:

If Ypres was the key of the Salient, Poperinghe was the key of Ypres, for the one main road that passed through its centre was the one and only way by which troops and transports could pass along to their destination, either line or Restwards. Strategically, of course it was of enormous importance, for here was the rail-head and here the centre of all this much fought-for portion of the Front. From the soldiers' point of view it was a city of refuge, where supplementary meals could be obtained and such amenities as Belgium could afford to its perforce occupants. It consisted of a handful of houses, clustering about two Churches, an Hotel de Ville, a square and one or two public buildings. Here, too, was Skindles and the Officers Club; with canteens of varying degrees of efficiency. And, above all, that remarkable institution born of the war, known as Talbot House, and now happily surviving as Toc H. Poperinghe was, of course, shelled very considerably by long range guns, for the Germans were not unmindful of its importance, the rail-head being a specially sought-out target for these occasions.

In *Adventures of a Despatch Rider*, Captain W. H. L. Watson remembers his trips to Poperinghe in 1915:

From Ypres the best road in Flanders runs by Vlamertinghe to Poperinghe. It is a good macadam road, made, doubtless by perfidious Albion's money, just before the war.

Poperinghe has been an age-long rival of Ypres. Even to-day its inhabitants delight to tell you the old municipal scandals of the larger town, and the burghers of Ypres, if they see a citizen of Poperinghe in their streets, believe he has come to gloat over their misfortunes. Ypres was self-consciously "old world" and loved its buildings. Poperinghe is modern, and perpetrated a few years ago the most terrible of town halls. There are no cocktails in Poperinghe, but there is good whisky and most excellent beer.

I shall never forget my feelings when one morning in a certain wine-merchant's cellar I saw several eighteen-gallon casks of Bass's Pale Ale. I left Poperinghe in a motor-ambulance, and the Germans shelled it next day, but my latest advices state that the ale is still intact.

Across the road from the wine-merchant's is a delectable tea-shop. Of Poperinghe I cannot speak too highly. There is a vast variety of the most delicious cakes. The proprietress is pleasant and her maids are obliging. It is also cheap. I have only one fault to find with it – the room is small. Infantry officers walk miles into Poperinghe for their tea and then find the room crowded with those young subalterns who supply us with our bully. They bring in bulldogs and stay a long time.

Dickebusch used to be a favourite Sunday afternoon's ride for the Poperinghe wheelers. They would have tea at the restaurant on the north of Dickebusch, and afterwards go for a row in the little flat-bottomed boats, accompanied, no doubt, by some nice dark Flemish girls. The village, never very pleasant, is now the worse for wear.

Lieutenant Francis Ledwidge, the Irish poet serving with the 1st Battalion Inniskilling Fusiliers, was encamped near *Brouwerij Het Zwijnland,* a local brewery, in July 1917 and was to write his poems *Home* and *Soliloquy* here. On 20 July, having just returned from a tour in the Pilckem trenches, he found a parcel with a copy of Katherine Tynan's book *Lord Edward* awaiting him. He immediately wrote a letter of thanks to her:

We have just returned from the line after an unusually long time. It was very exciting this time as we had to contend with gas, lachrymatory shells and other new and horrible devices. It will be worse soon. The camp we are in at present might be in Tir-na-n'Og, it is pitched amid such splendours. There is barley and rye just entering harvest days of gold, and meadows sweet rippling, and where a little inn In den Neerloop holds its gable up to the swallows, bluebells and goldilocks swing their splendid censers. There is a wood by where hips glisten like little sparks and, just at the edge of it, mealy leaves sway like green fire. I will hunt for a secret place in that wood to read Lord Edward. I anticipate beautiful moments.

Whether he ever read the book is unknown as he was killed near Boesinghe on 31 July.

In 1917, Lieutenant Edwin Campion Vaughan, 1/8th Royal Warwickshire Regiment. was encamped near St. Jan-ter-Biezen, a short distance to the west of Poperinghe. He reflected:

We were struck very soon by the different appearance of the landscape here. It was perfectly flat, devoid of trees or hedges and only relieved by compact, tangled hopfields. For a while we passed ruined brick houses, but later we came across little bungalows built entirely of packing cases and beaten out tins. After about an hour's march we came to a tiny village around which were clustered numerous canvas camps.

While walking with a friend from the camp to Poperinghe he noted:

We reached Pop at about 4 pm and found it a very busy little town. An incessant stream of motor-lorries, horses, limbers, guns and troops pours through its square, moving up and down the line. Nearly all the houses are empty but one or two shops are still open and do a great trade with the liberal Tommy.

It is well within range of Jerry's guns and the station and square receive frequent reminders of the fact. The old town hall on the corner where the road swings round to Ypres is now the APM's office and bears a huge black notice board which indicates whether the wind is 'SAFE' or 'DANGEROUS'. The church is damaged by shellfire, but mass is said there on Sundays.

After a preliminary wander around the town we went into a shop near the APM's office called Ypriana. We were surprised to find a large stock of English books and gramophone records, 'Swan' pens and all kinds of English goods, in addition to a splendid range of stationery and souvenirs. Five girls took turns serving in the shop, the eldest about 25. Two of them were twins and told me their parents had been killed by a shell some time before. In the square I saw a notice 'to the RC Chapel', and dragged Raddy down a little side street to a deserted convent. In the pretty chapel, with blue walls supporting clustered angels, we moralized aloud upon our presence in war-stained khaki on the spot where gentle nuns and children had knelt at benediction, their thoughts never straying to the possibility of an upheaval such as had now scattered them to different corners of Europe.

Lieutenant Edmund Blunden, Royal Sussex Regiment, billeted at 'M' Camp, also near St. Jan-ter-Biezen, in December 1916, recalled:

Our quarters were a set of huts and tents surrounding a small ugly farmhouse, a mile or less from the road to Poperinghe, with field paths leading past the biscuit-tin and sugar-box dwellings of refugees around it. Here we saw life in her rural petty beauties. The ploughman driving his share straight and glistening through the brown loam was a glory to see as we marched in the pale winter sun. We had eyes alike to see the curiosities of weathercocks, such as represented a running fox or a coach and horses, and to lift up our souls to the hills whereon a monastery towered. The spires were gilded with our unhoped-for emancipation, and the streets rang with our surprising steps.

Poperinghe was a great town then - one of the seven wonders of the world. The other six, indeed, were temporarily disregarded. Poperinghe streets are narrow, and there were thousands of soldiers there, coming and going; yet the town disappointed none, except when the enemy spoiled an afternoon with gas or long-range guns. One of our first impressions here was caused by the prominent notices against the Post Office concerning gas and the state of the wind; the skeleton of Ypres thus began to give us a nudge and a whisper. Meanwhile, we marketed and strolled about in contentment, allured from one shop window to another - all were bright (though splashed with mud from the columns of lorries), all were alive. If one could not buy a new razor, or a new cap, or O. Henry's works here, then Bohemia was nothing. The ladies spoke English with adroitness and amiable looks. Some observer preferred A la Poupée, the daughters of which tea house were certainly fair and gentle, the youngest 'Ginger' was daily attending school in Hazebrouck, a courageous feat. Ypriana also boasted some beautiful young persons who condescendingly sold gramophones, postcards of Ypres and fountain pens. Up in the higher windows, the milder air once or twice allowing, one saw old women making lace or some such thing. There was one church into which we could go, white walled and airy and cold, the delight of any who admired the Netherlands of the painters; another church in a tranquil side-street defied doubt with its strong and scarcely impaired tower.

American neuro-surgeon, Dr Harvey Cushing, based at a Casualty Clearing Station at Proven, made similar observations:

Pop is certainly a lively place these days, especially in the Grande Place, where we had to leave the car while we got lunch at the only place in the town where officers go - a place run by some refugee innkeepers from Ypres. All of the buildings except the few facing west were badly peppered, and there were occasional houses down. On one of the buildings was a large sign saying Wind Dangerous, and there was a big brass siren alongside of it to be used as an alert against gas. The place, of course, was infested with troops, and all the paraphernalia of war; and from the square led a narrow road with an arrow pointing east and a huge sign to Ypres.

Those citizens who, having originally left Poperinghe, chose not to live as refugees in their own country, returned to their homes to brave the shelling, pray for peace and hope to get rich quickly. For these, the fortunes of war could swing either way: to lose everything, or retain everything and gain more by supplying the soldiers' needs.

Louise Parmentier, one of many refugees in another not-so-soldier-populated town as Poperinghe, complained:

We were ruined. The people who could stay at home grew rich with the soldiers. The people who fled were always 'refugees'. It was a funny name. There is nothing you can do, you are ruined and still they talk about refugees.

When licences were issued to open shops in Poperinghe, refugees and the locals alike jumped at the opportunity to prosper. Apart from the centre of the town itself, every street that was used by soldiers moving in or out of the town was soon lined with makeshift buildings selling any legitimate or 'black market' commodity irrespective of what currency was in use. They accepted anything as long as it was money, and no doubt would have eagerly accepted the Deutschmark if the war so dictated. They had no scruples; if an item could not be acquired legally, it would be stolen from the military or from another source. In every street of the town there were shops, and houses, selling just about everything. One shop in Gasthuisstraat (now Shoe Post) advertised 'Postcards - Ruins of Ypres and Poperinghe - 1d each' along with washing soap, shaving soap, English cigarettes, cigars, toothpaste, chocolate, mirrors, polish, pipes, knives, candles and rosaries. The windows of the shop were crammed with these items and more - souvenir-brooches, cigarette-lighters, snuff-boxes, tie-pins, military buttons converted into lockets, handkerchiefs with popular songs printed on them – all so-called 'necessities'. The bijou store of Jules Depuydt (today's

Window shopping, military style

Capricio) specialised in fine jewellery, handcrafted shawls and tablecloths of Flemish lace whilst, on the market square, Andre Cossey's bazaar sold 'everything possible and impossible!' 24-hour old English newspapers - the Daily Express, Daily Sketch, Daily Mail and Daily Mirror, were sold by Henri Delboo-Wullemann in his shop at No. 72 Paardenmarkt – and an invoice discovered in the premises indicates that he had previously sold French newspapers.

Tubby Clayton, referring to the period in late 1915, commented:

The wealthier 'civil' population had moved into France, and the remainder, mainly refugees, were busily engaged in amassing wealth under circumstances adverse to the prosperity of their insurance companies. One combined pastry cook and brewery concern was said to have made £5,000 clear profit in four months.

Lieutenant-Colonel Frank Barry D.S.O., in Poperinghe in 1917, noted:

The town was absolutely swarming with officers and men of all possible arms. There were mess presidents and mess cooks buying provisions on their lawful occasions. There were officers visiting the Field Cashier. There were people going on leave or coming back, with no objection to wasting a few days. There was a large (more or less permanent) garrison and nearly always at least a Division billeted. Besides this there was always a mass of

May I go in?

people simply there for 'a day out'. The traffic passing through Poperinghe would have made Oxford Street in June look sleepy, and every lorry, limber, car or tender from whatever direction it was coming shed a few people more into the mass. There was no lack of wonderful enjoyments. For the officers the magnificent club started originally by Neville Talbot, and the famous crowded restaurants such as Cyrilles or La Poupée, known throughout the BEF as 'Ginger's'. Or you could have your hair cut in a shop which warned its customers laconically 'We do not work when the Germans are shelling'. You could buy all the things you had been needing for months - puttees and razors, shirts and studs and toothpaste. Expectant Subalterns could lay in an extra star. Colonels could get fresh supplies of ribbon. Other ranks knew well the best saloons for omelettes and vin blanc and chips. 'Silk Cards', too, you could buy, and passionate emblems of clasped hands and souvenirs innumerable. There were cinemas and 'shows' of various kinds besides the native picture-house and theatre. In a word the resources of civilisation left no dizzy joy to be desired.

Honourable Artillery Company Gunner W. R. Kingham M. A., wrote in his *London Gunners*:

There were various little shops about where Tommy was catered for, with pork-chops, eggs, and chips; but was there anywhere where one could get better fare? Cyril's (sic) Restaurant was reserved for officers – ugh! But the "British Hostel" – oh! We soon discovered that – a place where we were always welcome, and where a good appetising dinner was always obtainable. Men of our horse batteries used to come there too, and either in the kitchen or the bare room upstairs (for even here we must not trespass on officers' preserves), we would sit and feed joyously. Then to the pictures or some pierrot performance, or a visit to Talbot House, that most genuine of soldiers' homes. The quest – generally fruitless, except at Talbot House, where there was a great crush – for a cup of tea, and so back to sandwiches, shell-humping, a clearing to a flank.

With chips to follow

A cheery welcome from the shopkeeper

General Ponsonby of the 2nd Guards Brigade, was less enthusiastic:

I think this is the noisiest town I have ever been in. A regular train, not tram, runs down the narrow street in front of the house, and shakes the house as it passes, the engine screeching and whistling all day. Motor lorries are perpetually passing, also motor ambulances and motor bicycles all day and all night. Then comes a bouquet of shells to put the finishing touch on proceedings, also, on closer inspection, I find the town of Pop to be remarkably dull. The shops are all bun shops, sweets and French tobacco, the churches are shut although they open for Mass on Sundays so there is very little to do or see in the town.

Most of the troops sent home thousands of postcards, some humourous, some patriotic, many with romantic scenes and the text 'A Kiss From France'. Highly sought-after were those edged with 'real' Ypres lace and embroidered with 'real' silk by 'young girls whose loved ones were at the front'. The manufacturers, aware of their popularity, set up special assembly lines to satisfy the demand. These were preferred to standard-issue Field-Service Postcards, or 'quick-firers' as they were called, handed-out free of charge by the army. Remembering, Frank Richards said of these:

We simply wrote the address on them and signed our names and dates of sending on the backs; there was some printed matter on the backs such as 'I have been wounded' or 'I received your parcel', which we crossed out if it did not say what we wanted, simply leaving the words 'I am alright'.

While the civilian population were setting

NOTHING is to be written on this side except the date and signature of the sender. Sentences not required may be erased. If anything else is added the post card will be destroyed.

I am quite well.

I have been admitted into hospital
{ *sick* } *and am going on well.*
{ *wounded* } *and hope to be discharged soon.*

I am being sent down to the base.

I have received your { *letter dated_____*
{ *telegram „ _____*
{ *parcel „ _____*

Letter follows at first opportunity.

I have received no letter from you
{ *lately.*
{ *for a long time.*

Signature
only. }

Date_____

[Postage must be prepaid on any letter or post card addressed to the sender of this card.]

(25030) Wt.W3497-293 1,000m. 2/15 M.R.Co.,Ltd.

A 'Quick-firer'

up shops, cafés and estaminets, the army was setting up their own sorts of establishments.

A host of munitions dumps and supply depôts were sited in the Poperinghe area containing every calibre of shell and piece of equipment required by the modern army. Huge field kitchens continuously turned out thousands of meals for the ever hungry soldiers encamped nearby. Workshops, for the repair of guns and vehicles, were established throughout the region and, in 1916, No.29 Mobile Workshop, 1st Anzac Corps was set-up at Reninghelst while, in nearby Abeele, a Royal Engineers depôt saw working parties carrying all manner of materials up to the trenches, exposed to the dangers of enemy shellfire all the way. Working at a depôt had its advantages though, as Lieutenant John Aston reminisced:

> It was a real holiday. The men travelled to-and-fro by lorry, and in Abeele, the work was usually quite pleasant with jobs such as nailing duckboards together deliberately made as light as possible while the officer in charge could sit by a blazing fire in the officers' mess, or get a luxurious deep hot bath all by himself instead of squatting in a brewery tub with twenty others round him. The men too were often supplied with small luxuries for their meals.

Private W. W. Bell, M.M., 9th Battalion, Army Cyclist Corps, with an ammunition supply column moving from Poperinghe to Ypres, wrote:

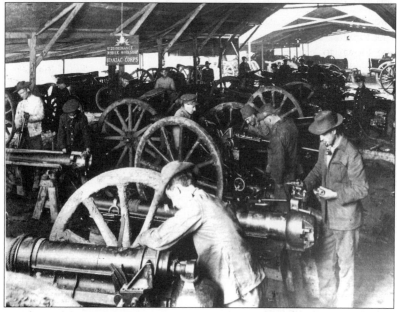

Australian workshop at Reninghelst

18

Directly it was getting dusk the ammunition column would start up and the GS wagons going up into Ypres with the rations for the troops up in the line. Then you could hear the wagon wheels starting on these cobbles, coming up and gradually getting louder and louder when they turned the corner. When the whole column of them was on the cobbles on the straight road into Ypres then old Jerry would open out with his long range guns and he'd get the range and drop shells along the road - one there, and one there, and one there - and then he'd come back again and work back and forwards all the time. All night that went on until it started the daylight. The road was absolutely a shambles with blood and gore and bits of horses, GS wagons with no wheels on, turned on their side, rations strewn right across the road. It was awful, really awful, and our orders were to shoot the drivers if they refused to stop so we could divide them up, so there was spaces in between. Directly they started to close up it only wanted a shell to drop on one and they'd all get it!

They did panic, you see. You get four mules in front of a GS wagon and these shells coming over, shrapnel up above, high explosive down below, and the noise! Deafening it was, and horses getting killed, and legs cut off, screaming. Of course, the drivers whipping them up wanted to get away, get off the road, get away from it, as quick as they can. Naturally - it's only human nature, isn't it? Want to get away out of that as fast as you can. Get up into Ypres. Our job was to stop them. It was a rotten job.

We were frightened ourselves. We were as frightened as them. Fear - you've got to be in it to understand what it means - really, fear is any moment to be blown to smithereens. These shells coming over one after another, screeching, one after another. You see, there was no other road into Poperinghe. It was the one straight road and old Jerry had the range of it to a 'T'.

In the early stages of the war the junctions of the numerous roads leading to and from the front became very congested with the vast numbers of army transports moving in and out of Poperinghe. All transports from the Channel Ports arrived in Poperinghe from the direction of Calais and Dunkirk via Roesbrugge–Proven–Westvleteren and International Corner, and from Boulogne and Le Havre via St. Omer–Steenvoorde–Abeele. They passed through the town's narrow winding streets via Casselstraat and Gasthuisstraat to cross the market square into Ieperstraat and onward to Ypres. It could take up to 15 minutes of waiting before being able to dash across the street. The noise would have been deafening - lorries of all sizes, G.S. wagons, caterpillar-tractors, ambulances, double-decker buses, artillery and ammunition limbers pulled by horses and mules, motorcyclists, bicyclists, cavalry units and marching troops.

In his book *Fireater*, Captain A. O. Pollard, V.C., M.C., D.C.M., described his experience of this in June 1915:

The Poperinghe–Ypres road was, as usual, crowded with traffic; troops in large and small parties, some in full equipment, some in light fatigue dress; limbers drawn by mules; endless ammunition columns; siege guns and howitzers; strings of lorries; motor cycle despatch riders; every conceivable branch of the Service was represented going about its business in orderly confusion. Even the cavalry who, since the inception of trench warfare, were rather out of fashion, had their part in the pageant.

In 1915, the Royal Engineers constructed a Switch Road to ease the congestion, linking Abeelseweg in the south via Zwijnlandstraat, Korte Werf, Diepemeers, St. Bertinusstraat, with Oostlaan in the north to form an effective bypass. By 1917, other bypasses were introduced around the town to ease congestion. A one-way system, and traffic segregation, successfully dealt with the problem, although it did little to help the worst congestion ever when, in mid-summer of 1917, over 500,000 soldiers passed through the town on their way to the front for Third Ypres.

Proven, a village west of Poperinghe, was billeted by the British Army after Second Ypres. A many-branched network of railway lines centred on Proven linked it with the Haringhe–International Corner–Boesinghe line, to the Field Hospitals at Westvleteren, and directly to Roesbrugge and Poperinghe. As Proven was considered to be relatively safe from enemy shelling, it's environs were used extensively for the storage of supplies and ammunition dumps. The village itself billeted troops. To ensure adequate accommodation was provided, it was the responsibility of a Billeting Officer to speak to householders, farmers, and landowners, and arrange for them to provide accordingly.

In his unpublished diaries, under the title *Rest Billets In Proven Area,* Lieutenant Walter-Laing wrote:

August 18th, 1917. Our Mess in Proven was the last house on the Dunkirk Road, after leaving the town. It was a substantial brick house with a sort of bridge from the front door to the causeway spanning a deep ditch. behind was a pleasant garden with a greenhouse. Our office was in the garden and was constructed from two Armstrong huts placed side by side. We had a very pleasant time here after the heavy work of the preceding months. The sleeping tents were in a meadow behind the garden. The Major General, and one or two of the senior officers had rooms in the house.

Proven consisted of one long paved street lined with brick houses, with a few large farmhouses and yards encircling it. At this time it was a busy rail-head, and thousands of men of the Army Service Corps and Chinese Labour Gangs were camped in the neighbourhood.

Due to the filthy conditions endured by the men in the trenches, personal hygiene figured highly on their list of priorities and, whilst it was possible to take a rudimentary wash in the trenches, nothing was more eagerly anticipated than the opportunity of a bath. Bathing for a soldier took on a variety of forms dependant on circumstance, from using a convenient river or stream, to having a bucket of water poured over him by an obliging comrade. In the early stages of the war some units even had mobile baths. Lieutenant Henry Lawson, then serving with the Manchester Regiment, recalls:

I cannot remember having a hot bath in a bathroom throughout my service overseas. However, I did have a portable canvas bath to hold a small quantity of hot water that was boiled by landladies and attended to by my batman. In a completely static sector of the line, when we held the trenches for eight days, we were entitled to use the facilities in the rear where the men could have shower baths. Sometimes the officers used these too.

Every battalion, after leaving the front, was obliged to bath collectively at the divisional baths. This provided the men with an almost 'normal' feeling, being able to wash off the accumulated filth, grime and stench of the trenches. In Poperinghe, not only was bathing a fairly safe business, but the baths were of a permanent nature - Rifleman. W. Worrell, 12th Battalion Rifle Brigade, describes a visit to the baths in a local brewery, the *Brouwerij Het Zwynland*:

There were three huge vats in the brewery and between them there were planks. The first vat was full of hot, dirty, soapy water. The next one had hot water, not quite so dirty. The last one had cold water, fairly clean. You started at one end and you stripped off. You tied your khaki uniform up in a bundle and tied your boots to it and your cap. Your underclothes were taken away to go in the fumigator, but it didn't usually do so. You went up and there were ropes across the vat, so you pulled yourself across on the rope to the other side, climbed out on to the next plank into the next vat, jumped in there, washed the worst of the dirt off, and then into the last vat. When you got out at the other end, you picked up a towel, wiped down and then looked around. 'Where's my hat?' It was the only way you could find your own bundle, with your hat and identity disc attached to it. Then you were issued with underclothes. If you were lucky you got some that nearly fitted you, but of course, I was the wrong size for that and it would always happen to me that I got huge underwear. They were all Long Johns in those days and by the time I'd done them up they were right around my chest, and I'd also have to take about three folds in the bottom of the legs. That would be topped by a vest hanging down below my knees. On the other hand, a fellow who was a six-footer would be issued with a set so small that he could hardly get into it at all, so we had to swop around as best we could.

Personal hygiene figures highly on their list of priorities

Sometimes the language got pretty fruity. We had some laughs. The odd thing is that you forget the bad times. It's the happy memories, the silly things that stick with you - like prancing about in that ridiculous underwear.

It was rumoured that the water in the third vat was as strong as the local beer. The origins of this belief are uncertain, but could possibly be attributed to Tubby Clayton who wrote:

We must not forget, in describing the amenities of the town, the system of half sealed streams, which having lost all sense of purpose or direction in the dark, devoted their powerful energies wholly to the culture of fever germs and mosquitoes. Out of these pure sources was pumped the brown bath water wherein we wallowed, and several experts aver that the resultant fluid was drawn off into casks and sold as Belgian beer. Other authorities deny this insinuation hotly, on the grounds that the confusion must have arisen through a similarity of taste alone.

Whatever the case, the vats returned to brewing beer each morning after bathing.

The Commanding Officer of the 1st Battalion Welsh Guards, when billeted near Poperinghe, was not over-impressed with the facilities, although it did not seem to concern the men:

This was the first time the battalion was actually in Poperinghe. One of the immediate duties was to get the men to the baths, and we find the Commanding Officer notes that they are "not to my mind satisfactory. Consist of two vats 10 feet by l0 feet and filled to a depth of 2 feet. The water is changed every two hours, and only one vat going at one time. They take 120 men an hour, so it means 240 men in same water – not sanitary or nice. They say not sufficient hot water to do more. I saw the washing of clothes arrangement. They first go through a disinfector, and then are dipped in creosote, so they should be all right."

The battalion being more or less clean, sought the amusements of Poperinghe the men at the canteens, the officers at "Ginger's," or a place run, we think, by a lady called "Kiki"; and everybody to the "Fancies."

In the morning there was drill, bombing practice, and route marches – the afternoons were mostly free. The square in the centre of the town was a scene of much movement both night and day. There was "tremendous traffic always going through, all military carts and limbers, and making a fearful clatter. Horses of all kinds – fierce ones, silly ones, and wise-looking ones with: Roman noses and hairy legs, and mules, absurdly like those in Punch, having jokes on their own. English soldiers in crowds, and a good many French."

The British Army's concern over the personal hygiene of its troops didn't go unnoticed by the Belgian population. A popular rhyme, reflecting their observations on the conduct of the allies, went:

> The Belgians curse and swear,
> The French eat and smear,
> The English wash and shear.

Every soldier who served in the line suffered with lice in the seams of shirts, underwear and uniforms. Captain Milne of the 4th Leicesters, spoke of these when returning to billets in Ouderdom:

... the battalion came out of the line and went back to rest at Ouderdom huts. It had been a long tour of duty, twenty eight days, and the battalion besides being very tired was very lousy. The "Chat," as the species of louse in question was called, was no respecter of persons. He paid his respects to the colonel; visited the adjutant; called on the company commanders; became attached to the platoon sergeants for rations, but not discipline; and fraternised only too freely with the rank and file. In some dug-outs men itched as soon as they sat down and as bathing facilities were entirely absent

Keeping clean was very important

in the trenches they had to be content to scratch. During the hot afternoons men could be seen solemnly sitting on the firing step stripped to the waist with their shirts on their knees, at which they made fierce and sudden dives with their fingers, and on being asked what they were doing they invariably answered in the same four words: "Having a chat up." The origin of this expression and for how many centuries it has been current in His Majesty's Forces appears to be unknown.

Various means were used by the men to rid themselves of these parasites. One way was to turn clothing inside-out, then hold the seams over a lighted candle, a popping sound as the lice and their eggs burst, being the desired result. Another was to heat a bayonet tip and run it along the seam. Lieutenant John Aston, possibly referring to the baths of *Brouwerij Six-Colpaert*, Reninghelstplein, wrote:

The men shed their underclothing and all went naked into a large shed full of open brewing tubs, where each man could get a hot bath; some preferred a hot shower under pipes pierced with holes. The steam was thick on these occasions. Then, opposite the entrance, into another shed where fresh underclothing was supplied, and as one can well imagine, large men often got shrunken garments. The clothing they had abandoned was all put into huge boilers where it was subjected to a very high steam pressure, by which all lice and other livestock were supposed to be killed, though many a louse seemed to enjoy the experience and came up to scratch again with a healthier appetite than ever.

Nurse Alison Macfie, serving near *Brouwerij Het Zwynland* in 1917, recalled:

The lane leading to the Hospital is easily called to mind and recognised by any old soldiers who have served in the area, as on one corner was the Military Laundry and on the other the De-Lousing Station. I shall never forget a visit we paid to the laundry and the sight of large heaps of socks in every stage of decay being turned over by two old women, who had picked out any that were capable of further use.

All this aside, Poperinghe was known to the troops as a place that offered more than just countless shops and bath-houses. It was better known for its estaminets, bars, restaurants, concert parties and the other amenities that a soldier liked to sample when he had the chance. Its reputation soon spread to divisions that had yet to pass through it, and throughout the British Army, bombing and shellfire apart, it became a place thought of as somewhere to visit with warm anticipation, if not pleasure.

In his book, *The Great War as I saw it*, Canon Scott, when reflecting on his time spent in Poperinghe was to say:

As one looks back to that period of our experience, all sorts of pictures, bright and sombre, crowd the mind – the Square at Poperinghe in the evening, the Guards' fife and drum bands playing tattoo in the old town while hundreds of men looked on, the dark station of Poperinghe in the evening, and the battalions being sent up to the front in railway trucks.

Edmund Blunden, when viewing the town from a distance, said of it:

Poperinghe again! even more divisional emblems, more badges and uniforms; more mud on the white house-fronts, more shutters up, fewer tiles on the roofs; the smell of petrol, veritably as sweet as life itself - we ask no violets yet. Through Poperinghe, among the wooden shops and taverns, to St.-Jans-ter-Biezen; a hopgarden or two, a shrine or two, peasants, dog-carts, poplars waving in the watery breeze. It is a real relief.

Lunch break

Bully Beef and biscuit,
Tea and grease combined
Make a British soldier
Think that he's just dined
Anon

3
FOOD & DRINK

L IFE FOR THE SOLDIER in or near the line was very much geared to things
that appealed to the outer senses: life; death; food; drink; cigarettes;
shelter; rest, and anything else that moved thoughts away from the
general unpleasantness of their life. A constant complaint amongst the
troops, apart from the pay and their leave, was food and drink or, more
specifically, the lack of it. Injustices in the distribution of leave, and the
seemingly unfair distribution of the bread and biscuit rations which the
infantry units of the front line suffered, were noticeably absent in the
transport and supply services. The differences enjoyed on a daily basis by
soldiers stationed in the area of Poperinghe, apart from causing much
friction and many brawls, developed an unhealthy attitude between them
and the infantry. Although many infantry camps were sited in the
Poperinghe area, leave for off-duty infantry was restricted. The military
population was made up of, primarily, men of transport and kindred
service, as well as those staffing the Casualty Clearing Stations surrounding
the town. Nevertheless, to all and sundry behind the lines, and especially
in such a well-populated area as Poperinghe, the major problem for the
military authorities in keeping the men partly satisfied, was drinking water.
   Extra water for laundry, cooking, washing and bathing, and the increase
in beer and tea consumption, took its toll on the normal sources. Local
wells were not only insufficient, but known to be infected with typhus.
Unwittingly, the soldiers had added to the problem by contaminating the
town water supply with their toilet and bathing habits. In August 1915,
during construction of the Switch Road, a bridge was built over the
Poperingsevaart behind which, by means of a lock-gate, a reservoir was
formed. Some distance down river, the Royal Engineers installed 12 huge
tanks to collect drinking water, and a well was sunk in the Paardenmarkt.
By August 1915, water-transports were being brought in daily from the
Mont des Cats and, shortly thereafter, from Roesbrugge where enormous
pumping and filtration systems had been installed in the river Yser.

Pumping water from the River Yser at Roesbrugge

Pumping water from outside a dugout on the outskirts of the town

Whereas Corps troops were soon satisfied with the water supply, that for the infantry was always in question, shortage or no shortage. Every man was ordered to fill his water bottle prior to going into the line, but was not permitted to drink except in an emergency, or when given express permission. Because of this it was not uncommon for men to carry two water bottles. Deemed ample to slake their thirst, though heavily tainted with chloride of lime, it was not unknown for a little to be saved for a rudimentary wash and shave. Due to the dangers of contamination, instructions were issued whereby under no circumstances was the water found in shell holes to be used for drinking purposes. Edwin Vaughan and his batman risked it in February 1917:

Dunham got a large chunk of ice out of a shell-hole behind us, so we had some milkless tea. I was a little dubious about using shell-hole water, but it was perfectly white and I should think any germs would be frozen.

Three months later he observed:

The one from which Dunham had got ice for our tea, was full of green water in which lay a rotting Frenchman - yet our tea had tasted quite good.

Frank Richards tells of another such incident:

A willow-ditch with about two feet of water in it ran from the enemy's trench through no-man's-land and through our trench; we drew water from it for drinking and cooking purposes. One night a patrol discovered some dead bodies lying in it. Orders were then issued that we were not to drink any more of the ditch water. But we still continued to drink it; our insides were now as tough as the outsides of our bodies.

Rum was a frequent issue in the trenches, particularly in cold or wet weather, and immediately prior to an attack. Transported in earthenware jars marked S.R.D., the initials of the Special Rations Department, the troops cynically chose to use their own interpretation – 'Seldom Reaches Destination', being the popular, if not accepted, meaning of the initials.

A popular 'ditty' with the infantry went:

> If the sergeants pinch the rum, never mind,
> If the sergeants pinch the rum, never mind,
> They're entitled to a tot,
> But they pinch the bloody lot,
> If the sergeants pinch the rum, never mind.
> If the sergeants pinch the rum, never mind.

Frank Richards recalls:

The rum came up with the rations and was handed over to the Company-Sergeant Major. If he liked his little drop he took his little drop; then the platoon sergeants would draw the allowance for each platoon, and they

Canadian troops having a snack with what appears to be their fair share of rum

A field kitchen in action

would take their little drops; sometimes the section corporals would draw their allowance from the platoon sergeants and by the time they had had their little sips there was damned little left for us. Sometimes platoon officers would issue it out and the majority I knew were very honest, but we had one in the Company who was a proper shark. His platoon sent up many prayers for his soul which were not answered. I have seen non-commissioned officers and men drunk in action, but it wasn't on their rum ration: it was rum they had scrounged from somewhere else. Our ordinary ration was very beneficial to us and helped to keep the cold out of our bodies – an extra drop made one reckless.

Being drunk in the trenches was a court martial offence, and a number of men of the 1st/5th Royal Warwickshire Regiment, unwittingly written about in *A Subaltern's War*, were lucky to have its author, Lieutenant Charles Edmonds (Charles Carrington), as their officer:

After a while Marriott came into the pill box grinning. I went out and found the ten ration carriers of last night all roaring drunk. The poor devils had got lost, just like everyone else, had wandered all night, and finally decided that the company was annihilated. Not without good sense they decided not to starve. They did their best with a whole company's rations, but a whole company's rum defeated them. Hither they had wandered very happy and very sleepy. We saved the rest of the food and rum, and sent over the remains, plenty for my handful of men. We brought most of them round to a condition soon where they could go back to the company. The hopeless cases we left to sleep it off.

Hot meals were prepared in Field Kitchens and, occasionally supplemented with cheese, hard-tack, biscuits and bread, delivered to the regimental camps for collection and distribution, frequently in metal containers or sandbags, to the men in the line. Frank Richards, continuing his grouse on army rations, continues:

Bread we never saw. There was no such thing as cooked food... we were lucky if we got our four biscuits a man daily, a pound tin of bully beef, and a small quantity of tea and sugar... a tin of jam between six... the jam was rotten and one firm that supplied it must have made hundreds of thousands of pounds profit out of it – the stuff they put in instead of fruit and sugar! One man swore that if he ever got back to England he would make it his first duty to shoot up the managing director and all the other heads of that particular firm. A tin of Maconochie's consisted of meat, potatoes, beans and other vegetables and could be eaten cold, but we generally used to fry them up in the tin on a fire. I don't remember any man ever suffering from tin or lead poisoning through doing them in this way. The best firms that supplied them were Machonochie's and Moir Wilson's, and we could always depend on having a good dinner when we opened one of their tins. But another

Preparing the rations

A Brigade bakery, preparing bread for the troops

firm that supplied them at this time must have made enormous profits out of the British Government. Before we ever opened the first tins we smelt a rat. The name of the firm made us suspicious. When we opened them our suspicions were well founded. There was nothing inside but a piece of rotten meat and some boiled rice. The head of that firm should have been put up against the wall and shot for the way they sharked us troops... Iron rations were carried in case of an emergency but were never supposed to be used unless orders came from our superior officers... Each man was his own cook and we helped our rations out with anything we could scrounge.

In the line, officers' meals were little better. Lieutenant Mottram recalls:

I got into the dug-out and took my first bite since noon. It was nearly midnight. Eaten by the reflection of the enemy's flares in the stagnant water outside, it consisted of bully beef dug out of the tin with my knife, bread that had fallen into various shell-holes from darkness and fatigue, if he had not been hit, and which therefore tasted of the contents of shell-holes, that is human remains, various chemicals, excreta, well-manured Belgian farm soil, and rain-water – and, to finish with, cheese that survived it all.

Edwin Vaughan was less specific:

... a cold chunk of doubtful steak – covered with muddy whiskers of sandbag, followed by a tin of peaches, rain-soaked bread and sandbaggy cheese, some cold tea out of a petrol can.

A canteen just behind the lines

Officers having a quick snack in the reserve line

A 'red-cap' trio at lunch

When not in the line, and for those who never entered the line at all, there were the Canteens. Captain Dunn remembers the one he used:

Ours was the cheapest canteen of its kind. Slices of cake, a cup of tea or coffee, and 'coolers' were very profitable at a penny. Tobacco, biscuits, sausages, chocolate and some other articles in large demand were brought from the makers and sold at shop prices. Other goods with a steady sale were sauces, meat and fish pastes, and milk in tins, sardines. Sales showed queer vagaries of taste.

Every soldier, once out of the trenches, would have a hot meal fairly high on his agenda, and meals at camp were not what he had in mind. In Poperinghe, officers dined on chickens, steaks and oysters, drinking fine wines, champagnes and watered-down, 'baptised' spirits. Other ranks had omelettes and chips, with beer or cheap wine. Spirits were limited to 'café-cognac', 'café-avec-lait-brun' (with whisky) and 'vin blanc ecossais', better known as 'white wine with a nod' (again with whisky)'

On the outskirts of the town, in the area of Hoograaf there were a number of eating and drinking places much frequented by the troops. One of them, *De Herzog van Brabant*, well-known by other ranks for its flowing beer and rowdy evenings, caused some concern to the military authorities. Although this area was the furthest extent of the Town Major's jurisdiction, it did not stop him from taking a particular interest in the landlord of *De Herzog van Braban*t. On more than one occasion the place was closed down. There were strict opening hours for civilians and soldiers, and when a bar was placed out-of-bounds it could remain so for anywhere between 14-days to 6-months. The Military Police showed no leniency with Belgian bar owners as they were in competition with the Forces Canteens, and British army inspectors regularly took samples of the beers and wines, accepting only the highest of standards. The sale of wine was totally forbidden, and beer bottles were not allowed as soldiers could 'take them away', but there was nothing they could do to stop *De Herzog van Braban*t remaining at the top of the soldiers' lists for favourite bars.

In Poperinghe, almost every house had its regular visitors for omelettes or fried eggs and chips. These simple meals were just what the infantryman wanted after his fare in the trenches. To him, it did not matter that his source of a hot drink, fried food and café-cognac, might be the kitchen of a partially destroyed farmhouse, a cottage or an earthen-floored hut made out of packing cases. Appearance was immaterial, pleasure was everything.

In Denis Waters' book *Death's Men*, F. Voigt is quoted as saying:

We entered the estaminet. Soldiers were standing round the walls waiting for vacant seats. An oil lamp was hanging from the ceiling. In the middle there was a long table and soldiers seated around it, squeezed tightly together,

Troops eating in the open at camp

Troops lining up for food at a hutted camp

eating eggs and chips, drinking wine and coffee. The air was hot and moist and smelt of tobacco, burning fat and steaming clothes. There was a glowing stove at one end of the room. It looked like a red-hot spherical urn on a low black pedestal. A big bowl of hot fat was seething on it. A woman with flaming cheeks was throwing handfuls of sliced potatoes into it while she held the saucepan in which the eggs were sputtering. The conversation was boisterous and vulgar, much of it at the expense of the woman. She laughed frequently, pretending to be shocked, and called the soldiers 'naughty boys'.

Speaking of her experience at the time Bertha Tally remembers:

Madame Maria always had soldiers in the house for eggs and chips. Some of them were only boys and called her Mother but most of them called her Marie. She had a huge vat that she used to cook the chips in and if it was fine she cooked outdoors which the soldiers enjoyed immensely. If they didn't have any money she would accept lumps of coal from the steam vehicles as payment. My eldest brother used to help mother with the cooking and one time he tripped and fell into the vat of hot fat. He was badly burned and the soldiers took him to Remy Camp where the doctors looked after him until he was better. Mother always used to say, "If you have a potato and an egg in the house, you will always have a meal on the table".

If the private houses of Poperinghe did a good trade, then the cafés and estaminets did even better. There were many to choose from, and each developed its own regular clientele. *In de Vier Gekroonden* in Boeschepestraat (now the Hotel Kring), was the British Officers' Hostel, said to be the best, cheapest, liveliest and oldest. On a visit there in 1917, Edmund Blunden recounts:

I chose a little table in the 'British Hostel' where the gramophone was chiefly employed on a minuet by Boccherini and something 'Hawaiian' - not bad accompaniments (for the uncritical young) to Madame's chickens and wines.

The market square was full of popular establishments patronised by NCO's and other ranks: *A La Fontaine*, (today's Du Tram), *A St Laurent* (now De Hopbeurs), *Au Casino*, (now Juwelen Rubrecht) and *A La Fabrique*, retaining the Flemish version of its name today – 't Fabriekje, and one of the few establishments to retain its original facade. At the end of the Garenstat, behind what is now 'Oud Vlaenderen', there was a small café/bazaar called *In de Maan*, and on the corner of Veurnestraat the 'In den Nieuwen Haene' was then the estaminet *In den Ouden Haan*, which the French named *Au Coq*, and, at No. 35, *L'Epée Royale*, today's 'Tandarts Alphonse Degroote-Garmyn'. Standing on the corner of the square and Gasthuisstraat, retaining its original name today, is the *Café de la Paix*.

Captain Dunn was to write of this area as:

From the earliest days there were restaurants and estaminets for all ranks and purses. A few estaminets which had a piano got a running start in the Army's favour. The piano attracted men with parlour tricks. In amusing themselves they drew so much custom that men waited outside to get in, or just to listen. The performers were inspirited and repaid by the house with free drinks; they were also bidden to wait within hail of the back door until the Police had made their rounds, and were then given supper. Everything was free-and-easy; there was no programme, but there were few intervals. A song with a chorus was most thought of; the words, the voice, might matter little. Topical improvisations of four or eight lines, with a climax repeatable only in convivial company, passed into circulation.

For those 'with rank and purse' a totally different Poperinghe eating-style was available, as the meal Dunn enjoyed in Poperinghe suggests:

... hors-d'ouevres, clear oxtail soup, fresh whiting, dressed cutlet and celery, stuffed turkey and trimmings, plum pudding, angels on horseback, dessert - apples, oranges, dates, walnuts: Veuve Cliquot, Kümmel, coffee. The turkey at 3s.2d. per lb., cost 30s. I don't suppose anything like the dinner could be got at home.

Generally speaking the officers did very well for themselves. Major Francis Graham, Royal Field Artillery wrote home:

I am sorry you should have a wrong impression about the food; we have always had more than enough, both to eat and to drink. I give you a day's menu at random. Breakfast - Bacon and tomatoes, bread, jam and cocoa. Lunch - Shepherds Pie, potted meat, potatoes, bread and jam. Tea - Bread and jam. Supper - Oxtail soup, roast beef, whisky and soda, leeks, savoury, coffee (Savoury alternates with rice pudding and stewed fruit).

We have provided stores of groceries and Harrod's have been ordered to send us out a weekly parcel. However, if you would like to send us out an occasional luxury it would be very welcome. There are four chief events every day. They are Breakfast, Lunch, Tea, Dinner. We are feeding very well. I enclose tonight's menu:-

Soupe, Queue de Boeuf a la Harrod's
Roast Mutton a la Gouvernement
Vegetables ad lib
Apple Tart a la Bailleul with Cream
Sausage Roll a la Chef (i.e Home Made)
Fromage, Biscuits a la Bain d'Oliver
Confiture
Dessert - Apple and Grapes;
Café.

L'Espérance, or 'Hope' as the name literally translates, was nicknamed 'What Hopes?' by the troops. Now owned and operated by Filip and Leila

Vanspranghe, it retains both its original name and little-changed frontage. In 1927, Henry Williamson, on his pilgrimage to the old battlefields with an ex-tank officer he chose to call 'Four-toes', well documented in his book, *The Wet Flanders Plain*, returned to Poperinghe and, dining at *L'Espérance*, found its proprietor, a certain Auguste Dezutter-Leroy, offering a completely different service to that offered during the war:

… we left to seek a meal in some less splendid, and doubtless less expensive, place. … we counted our money; we had about seven pounds between us. It was not very much. Still, man must eat and drink. We sought a cheap estaminet.

In the rue d'Hôpital we found what looked like a cheap place. We entered, and out of a dark kitchen came, in due course, a young and comely woman with a reserved and pleasant smile on her countenance. We asked for an omelette. Toute de suite! Chairs were piled on the long table inside, on which lay a soiled and worn American cloth.

We waited half an hour. The room was dreary and lifeless. Should we walk out? It looked perhaps too cheap a place. But no; we might disappoint the young woman with the Mona Lisa smile.

We waited. A smell of burning stole into the room. Still, it might be only the egg-shells. Then came the young woman, with the same fixed and pleasant expression, bearing a yellow and black omelette. She put it before us, with slices of bread. We asked for butter. Butter? Yes, butter. Toute de suite. We scraped off the unburnt part of the omelette, washing it down with a bottle of ordinary cheap white wine. Ah well, it didn't pay always to be too economical.

Two Belgian shop assistants entered, and were served with soup and roast chicken. We eyed that chicken, thinking philosophically that beggars have to be choosers. That lunch would cost them ten francs each, at least!

The butter arrived, about two pounds of it, at the end of the meal. Then Four-toes, wishing to overcome his inferiority-complex about the language, boldly asked for 'l'addition.' He was beckoned outside, semi-mysteriously, by the Mona Lisa wench. He went through the door into the café. When I joined him a moment later, he was counting the change from a hundred franc note. Forty francs left out of it! Seeing his expression of doubt, the patron leaned over his money box, while Mona Lisa stood by his side. "I can't quite make out what the old blighter's saying," muttered Four-toes. "The change seems wrong, somehow." "Monsieur," said the patron, "Inside, eating my best chicken, are two Government officials. There is a large tax on strangers having meals in Belgium just now. C'est la guerre, m'sieu. So, monsieur, to save you the expense of the tax, I call you out here and you pay me secretly. Messieurs, don't forget the waitress."

Mona Lisa held out her hand. Feebly I gave her five francs, while the consumed part of the omelette turned to hard lumps, like shrapnel bullets, inside me. Sixty francs for luncheon! And the combined bill at the Hazebrouck hotel for supper, bed, and breakfast, was less than that.

Outside, we looked at the name of the place. A L'Espérance! "What hopes," as we used to say.

We laughed, and for some kilometres along the road to Ypres, were withering the patron, or his detachable wraith accompanying us, with ironical speeches. Sixty francs! "It was just the same during the War," said Four-toes cynically. "They always got what they could out of the troops. Money is first, everywhere, every time".

Immediately next door to *L'Espérance,* today's De Ranke is a popular café/restaurant/patisserie. During the war, named *La Poupée,* the soldiers referred to it as 'Ginger's', the front being an estaminet/bar with the rear section serving as a dining room. Elie Cossey, the proprietor, a shoemaker by trade, was a renowned wit, a practical joker and a shrewd businessman. He saw the opportunity for a flourishing business the moment large numbers of troops began arriving in the town and immediately designated his establishment as a place of entertainment for officers only. He secured a regular supply of spirits, at the time not only illegal, but virtually impossible to obtain elsewhere. He also boasted one of the best stocked wine cellars in the Ypres Salient. It was said the popping of champagne corks on any evening drowned out the sound of the guns in the Salient. This claim was given credence when, during renovations in recent years, thousands of champagne corks were found between the ceiling joists. He also provided good meals at affordable prices, but his *tour de force* was his three beautiful daughters. The youngest, Eliane, nicknamed 'Ginger', was slim and the most attractive of the three. When the British arrived in Poperinghe she was 13-years old and said to be 'wise beyond her years'. The other two, Martha and Marie-Louise, did not share the same adulation afforded their younger sister of whom it was reported 'men of all nationalities came from miles around to see this stunning continental beauty'.

Tubby Clayton wrote of *La Poupée*:

In late 1915 two of the four chief restaurants were already in full swing... that in the Rue de Boeschepe (British Officers Hostel). A la Grande Poupée behind a shop in the Square, where the thirteen-year old schoolgirl 'Ginger' had already established her fame. Any defects in the cuisine or in the quality of the champagne were more than compensated by the honour of being chosen as her partner in the exhibition dance that she gave with the utmost decorum as the evening drew on.

Major Dudley-Ward, DSO, MC, Royal Welch Fusiliers noted:

Poperinghe possessed a few simple pleasures which cheered the soldiers' hearts. Talbot House (Toc H) has its place in history, but so, too, has Ginger's restaurant. The latter drew its name from a girl of, perhaps, twelve or thirteen years old, a carroty-haired, sharp-tongued little wretch who delighted in chaff. There were other restaurants, but none so celebrated as Ginger's. There were shops, and in the evening concert parties – nothing of any real merit, but the Army, generally, had a great affection for 'Pop'.

It was not unknown for Elie Cossey to arrange for his customers the appearance of a *guest artiste*, invariably a provocative and scantily clad mademoiselle moving amongst the men singing *Un Peu d'Amour.*

Captain Dunn, also a regular client there, wrote:

November 25th 1917. Dining at La Poupée, I contrasted the abundance of food in this part of 'poor Belgium' with the meagreness and makeshift at home. Dinner costs 4/-: a good soup, whiting, roast chicken and potato, cauliflower au gratin, coffee, bread, butter, sugar without limit - no margarine, saccharine or other substitutes as at home. London can't offer anything like it. There was also a large choice of wines at quite moderate prices.

Edwin Vaughan went there on 29 July 1917:

La Poupée in its new role as a lingerie shop in the immediate post-war years

Young 'Ginger' ...

Our next visit was to a café in the Square - La Poupée. The two rooms were full of diners but we found a table in the glass roofed garden. A sweet little sixteen year old girl came to serve us. I fell victim at once to her long red hair and flashing smile. When I asked her her name, she replied 'Gingair' in such a glib way that we both gave a burst of laughter. We had a splendid dinner, with several bottles of bubbly, and Ginger hovered delightfully about us. Over cigars and liqueurs I offered her my heart, which she gravely accepted. At 10.30 we rose to leave, and at that moment everybody ducked at the whizz of a shell which burst outside. Then another went into the station, and as we walked home we heard them falling all over the town. Still more did we marvel at the pluck of these young girls who were carrying on in such danger.

His interest seemed to go beyond just 'marvelling at the pluck':

July 31st. At about 6.30 a notice was posted in the mess room that owing to the shelling, dinner would not be served at the club. So I went along to La Poupée and placed myself in the dainty hands of Ginger.

On 10 August, arriving at Le Havre from leave in England he:

... caught a train at 11 am. from which at 5 pm. I alighted to turn my steps to La Poupée once more. Ginger was sweet to me and gravely listened to all my talk of home and England, in return informing me that life in Poperinghe was becoming more hectic. Shelling was heavier and officers much more badly behaved. Every night there was a small riot when drinks had been flowing, and through it all the guns and the troops rolled steadily through the town to Ypres.

August 11th. Returning to Poperinghe, we had dinner at La Poupée where Ginger told us (in strict confidence) that there would be a big advance in less than a week. This, by the way, is the first rumour we have heard.

Prior to moving up to the front he went to *La Poupée* for dinner:

August 13th. We had a most wonderful meal with many drinks so that when we started back through the darkness, we were all a little unsteady.

After the war 'Ginger' married a British

... an older 'Ginger' ...

officer and went to live in England, but the marriage failed and she returned to live in Poperinghe. Her sister, Marie-Louise also married a British officer, a Captain John Reynolds, attached to the Chinese Labour Corps. The wedding was a lavish affair and, in keeping with military tradition, two rows of fellow officers, with swords crossed aloft, formed an arch for the couple. Outside, rice was thrown over the couple which the local citizenry found both wasteful and incomprehensible. Reynolds had billeted frequently in the small bazaar belonging to Andre Cossey (now Apotheek Van Nielandt-Ermens), a few doors away from *La Poupée*. After the wedding and after his leaving the army, he and Marie-Louise settled near Ostend. During the mid '20s they returned to Poperinghe to take over the shop that had once been his billet.

At No. 16 Gasthuisstraat, a large hotel, *A la Bourse du Houblon*, was for 'Officers only'. It was owned and run by a widow, Madame Emma Bentin-Derycke, helped by her three daughters, Zoe, Lea and Marie. It became known as *Skindles*. The change of name occurred during early 1916, although the exact circumstances are not too clear. Locally it is said that a British officer likened it to the riverside hotel in Maidenhead which belonged to his family. Henry Williamson's account of its naming, reads:

> In June, 1916, an officer in the Rifle Brigade, enjoying eggs and chips and a bottle of wine in a certain estaminet in Poperinghe, declared to his friends that it was as good a pub. as Skindles at Maidenhead. The estaminet had already a longish name painted on its front – Hotel de la Bourse du Houblon something or other – but no one took any notice of that. The British officers began to call it Skindles, and very soon the three rooms on the ground floor were crowded with tables, and the tables with bottles; and around the bottles (for the water of the country was condemned for drinking purposes) sat the British officers smoking, laughing, eating, or wanting to eat, and Shouting the name of Zoe, which was the name of the daughter of the "Mother of the Soldiers," as madame was called. The officer of the Rifle Brigade was killed on the Somme a few weeks later, as were nearly all of his friends; but others came, and vanished, and others after them; and many, many more stretched their booted and puttee'd legs under the tables, and drank in a fug of tobacco smoke and laughter; until the guns were silent and the feet of men marching at night were rarely heard, and upon the "Mother of the Soldiers" and her helpers fell a strange loneliness.

> And now it is the Hotel de la Bourse du Houblon something or another again, having returned to its former easy comfort and prices. You may drink vin blanc there at 2d. a glass, and play billiards, or a game of violent cannons off inelastic cushions, in the second room; but you cannot get eggs and chips any more, or biftecks and French mustard. If you ask for these things in your halting French they will refer you to the Hotel Skindles up the street,

which occupies the large corner house once holding the Officers' Club. There is a booklet of photographs about it, showing the Smoking Room, A Dinning (sic) Room, and The Park (complete with two genuine shell-holes and some dud aerial torpedoes). And there is, according to the booklet, yet another Skindles in Ypres, opposite the station, with nearly fifty large windows along its front, blazoning its name in huge gilt letters on its brow. "Most modern and up-to-date hotel in the salient (sic) Home Comforts, Reading Room Baths – Hot and Gold (sic) English speaking staff."

Bairnsfather himself could not have limned so exquisite a Soldier's Dream ten years ago. Gold baths in Ypres! Colossal offspring of the demure little Hotel de la Bourse du Houblon something or other in the rue d'Hôpital. Such is the fortune of War; but the little anonymous subaltern of the R.B.'s, now a flower-girt headstone with the plain inscription "Known Unto God" somewhere in a cemetery of Picardy, is not forgotten by the "Mother of the Soldiers."

Emma Bentin and her daughters, opened a second establishment at No. 57 Gasthuisstraat, naming it *Skindles Hotel*. Throughout the remainder of the war it was as equally well patronised as the *Skindles* at No 16 and became Poperinghe's 'official' Officers' Club.

Colonel M.C. Clayton D.S.O. D.L, of the Cambridgeshires was to say:

Whenever opportunities occurred, I encouraged officers and men to go to Poperinghe, where the former could dine at Skindles and visit the club or attend the performances at the theatre, and the latter had a choice of Divisional Concert Parties, many of which reached a high standard of excellence. Moreover, all ranks were sure of a welcome at any hour, day or night, at Talbot House (Toc H, a name now known all over the world). Regimental officers were, however, always faced with the difficulty of getting the rank and file transported from the camps to the town. In this respect, I think our Staff lacking in sympathy and enterprise. The strain of war was infinitely greater on the fighting branches of the army than on departmental corps living in back areas. Consequently greater facilities should have been afforded them for transport. I know that there were many obstacles in the way, but they should, and could, have been overcome.

In *Nomad Under Arms*, Ben Assher, serving with the artillery, wrote in his own way of the delights of eating at the Officers' Club in Poperinghe:

Poperinghe officers' club I name in passing, not with intent to paint you any special picture but with the wish to make you some small subscription to the theme of such amenities throughout the B.E.F. in general. Who was responsible for the inauguration of these pleasant hospices it is impossible for me to say, not knowing; but I would fain remove the hat proverbial to the fellow and I should bow according, also, if I met him.

As a resort wherein a state reflecting something of the outer world was met the officers' club proved havens for lorn and lone, and cheerful refuges for many.

For it was here the fowl, well roasted in the simple way, and served with welcome tribute of good French or Flemish cress and lettuce, savoured to those who'd lived for long on "bully" in the trenches, or at the best been favoured with the British ration – rendered 'a la Britannique (very) by a selected army henchman – savoured, I'd say, as portion fit for ancient Princes, seated before the crude, mediaeval board with sundry minions, dames and vassals.

... Moreover, within the atmosphere of such a hostelry there used to reign, more especially at night, a brisk conviviality which differed in the main from that more often met in pre-war messes, mainly because of the assorted types unstandardised to martial pattern, and as a consequence of parties generally not knowing one another. Yes it was quite a pleasant interlude the place provided, and a most refreshing contrast to the daily scenes of modern battle.

Today, nothing remains of the original *Skindles* that once was the establishment at No. 16 Gasthuisstraat, Poperinghe. Taking its place is the red brick facade of the chemist's, Kestelijn.

No. 57, although no longer *Skindles Hotel,* retains its grandiose exterior. and heavy front door.

Entertainment at the Officers' Club

Take me further back in time to the Chorus Line.
Down where the footlights shine, the Chorus Line.
Grease painted and glad ragged 'til dawning
Pale faced and dressed to kill by morning.
Jim Boyes

4

CONCERT & CABARET

EQUALLY AS IMPORTANT as food, drink and leave to the soldier was the sort of entertainment he could find in what little spare time he enjoyed. In 1915 Tubby Clayton said:

There was a canteen in the Square, run by a Wesleyan chaplain, but beyond this nothing but refugee shops, bright behind their rabbit-wire windows. Of course, there were estaminets everywhere, good bad and of all intermediate complexions. The town, at the time, was intermittently shelled but 'nothing to write home about'. Some very heavy 'Stuff' had come in during the early summer when the fashionable area of the town was constantly changing. One large shell had completely demolished the original English Church house near the square. Poperinghe itself consists of a Grand Place preternaturally broad, and five streets preternaturally narrow. You could scarcely shout across the square; you might all but shake hands across the streets.

This was soon to change and, complementing the estaminets, shops, restaurants, and cafés catering for both officers and men alike, Poperinghe saw the opening of concert halls and cinemas, plus a theatre, today's National Hop Museum. These became popular and were regularly packed with soldiers. The *Palace Cinema (today's* Hotel Palace), frequently showed westerns and Charlie Chaplin films. In *The Coliseum* (now Hotel Belfort) on the market square, the silent films were accompanied by Yvonne Battheau on piano. There was also a cinema in a large hop warehouse near the station which has since been demolished.

Certain officers were well aware of the need for their men to take a break from the routine of military life and take advantage of what Poperinghe had to offer. In his *Field Guns in France*, Lieutenant-Colonel Neil Frazer-Tyler D.S.O., T.D., R.A. (T.A.) wrote of one such officer:

On 3rd September 1917 some general became obsessed with the notion that the Royal Regiment needed washing, not of the laundry type, but in respect of the corpus file, so each battery was offered twenty-four hours out of

47

action to carry it out... they were all given passes to go off and play in Pop, and wash if they wanted to, while the double issue of rum and cigarettes kept the remnant of the army content at the wagon line, it made quite a pleasant break... At Pop we found the usual huge crowd in the street, a band in the square, a few shells flying about, and both clubs filled with friends. After dinner there, having dismissed the car, we "long-hopped" the eight miles back to our wagon line.

Almost without exception every division had its own Concert Party composed of men who, in many instances, had no other responsibility than to provide entertainment in the camps and towns behind the lines. This was much sought after work, as they were allotted extra leave to visit the music halls and latest revues in England to gather new material. Virtually every Concert Party in the British Army performed in the town at some time during the war. Prior to their enlistment, many of the performers had been household names in civilian life and were especially popular with the troops. Every Concert Party had a name in some way associated with its division or make-up of regiments within the division. *The Balmorals* of the 51st (Highland) Division, *The Red Roses* of the 55th (West Lancashire) Division, *The Jocks* of the 15th, *The Tykes* of the Yorkshire, *The Bow Bells* of the 56th, *The Shrapnels* of the 33rd, *The Roosters* of the 60th, *The Crumps* of the 41st, *The Eighty Eights*, *The Whizzbangs* and *The Duds* of the Field Artillery. The nurses at l'Hôpital Elizabeth had their own troupe named *The VA Dears*, the Chinese Labour Corps had theirs, *The Tsjings,* and the 4th Australian Division came in with *The Smart Set*. Posters around Poperinghe advertised familiar sounding place names and acts and The Empire Theatre showed a permanent poster announcing 'Always Something New'.

Captain Dunn after an evening at *The Alhambra* commented:

The Pedlars', said to be the best Divisional company in the town, played to a full house: seats 1 and 2 francs. Topical skits were followed by 'Buckshee', a revue mostly lifted from 'Topsy Turvy'. 'The Leave Boat' and 'The Garden of Eden' were good scenes: the 'girl's' arms gave him away.

He also saw the 4th Division Concert Party, *The Follies*:

... the model on which all other divisions formed a troupe of entertainers assisted by two Parisian ingenues whom the BEF called 'Vaseline' and 'Lanoline': after a few weeks their parts were taken by female impersonators.

Such was the influence of *The Follies* and the popularity of 'Vaseline' and 'Lanoline' that the 6th Division incorporated them into their *The Fancies* Concert Party.

The 2nd Leinster Regiment's Captain F. C. Hitchcock recalled:

The concert troupe consisted of nine artistes and two girls. The latter were known as 'Glycerine' and 'Vaseline'. One was a refugee from Lille, and the other was the daughter of an estaminet keeper at Armentières. The most priceless turn in the show was the singing of 'I'm Gilbert the Filbert' by one of these wenches who could not speak English.

H. H. Morell wrote:

I saw them in Poperinghe and the stars were two buxom, bonny girls. They couldn't sing, act, etc. but who cared! They were well guarded and never seen off stage." They were later joined by a third 'Gasoline' who like 'her sisters' could neither dance, act, nor sing; but, despite their shortcomings as performers they added feminine interest to the shows purely by virtue of the fact that they were said to be women.

In 1916 Mottram watched *The Follies*:

... a pierrot entertainment enlivened by two ladies in the caste. I believe that originally they were local girls, but their places were taken by male impersonators, and the names, Lanoline and Vaseline, with which they had been christened, gave way to Ack Emma and Pip Emma. I have heard 'The End of a Perfect Day' and 'Old Roger Rum' sung since that time without being able to account for the delight I then experienced.

With a lack of female talent to draw on, men undertook the feminine rôles in the majority of Concert Parties. Sometimes, as Lieutenant Walter-

The Balmorals of the 51st (Highland) Division

Laing of the Coldstream Guards recalls, with great success:

Last night I went to a splendid concert given by the 3rd Bn. who are living in the same camp as the 2nd Bn. This concert was a sort of Revue, - with Cinderella as a sort of excuse. The two ugly sisters were represented, and an officer acted the Prince. Cinderella was a private soldier who made a splendid woman and sang falsetto magnificently. Then there was a ballet dancer in frilly skirt and tights who was simply great. The whole thing was an excuse for one song after another, which had nothing to do with Cinderella of course. There were also two funny men whose jokes were not fit for ladies to hear.

Often, as Fusilier Eric Hiscock, remembers, in unexpected ways:

What astonishes me is the way the two 'females' engendered excitement among their rude and rough male audiences. Why did those Fusiliers, not long out of the line, fight for seats near to the improvised stage? To be near enough to detect the rouged and powdered cheeks that a few hours earlier had been shaved with an Army razor? To decide that the swelling bosoms under the flimsy dresses were false, and that above those twinkling, black-stockinged legs was a sex-organ that could have differed from anything they had only in size? Judging from the way they sat and goggled at the drag on stage it was obvious that they were indulging in delightful fantasies that brought to them substantial memories of the girls they had left behind them in... wherever. As the Quarter-master Captain lisped after performing before a particularly rapt audience: 'I bet there were more standing pricks than snotty noses tonight.' Astonishingly, I suspect he was right.

The Fancies probably spent longer in Poperinghe than any other troupe, during which time they were billeted in the Town Theatre in Casselstraat. Besides staging music hall and variety shows here, they were regularly called upon to give performances in a makeshift theatre in a large building to the left of the station, used briefly between 1915 - 1916 to billet up to 1,000 men at a time. The building itself became known as *The Fancies*.

Edmund Blunden spoke of it as:

By the station, in a brick storehouse among many spacious buildings belonging to the hop-factors, the 'Red Roses' in song and dance never ceased to gild the clouds of fate. The simple legend 'BOX OFFICE' had its epic majesty, and one still sees the muddy track leading thither across the railway as the high road to Parnassus, and hurries to the feast.

Tubby Clayton dubbed *The Fancies*:

A Great Divisional Show justly celebrated for Fred Chandler's tenor voice, Dick Horne's 'Rogerum' (a coon song version of the Parable of Dives and Lazarus, with a magnificently onomatopoeic chorus, which lifted the Sixth Division along over many miles of mud).

Rifleman H.E. Lister, 12th Battalion The Rifle Brigade, remembers a concert party performed in the vicinity of Poperinghe:

It meant a lot to us when we came down the line, because there was nowhere to go, you see, it was all desolate. It made a great difference to the troops, though of course a lot of the troops didn't think of anything more than going in the estaminet and getting a drink. Captain Gilbey started the 'Very Lights' and he had men out of the whole division. When they weren't acting at night, they were doing such jobs as taking up the rations. They didn't go actually fighting, but they were all serving soldiers. There was one number that always used to bring the house down, and they always sang it. It was called 'Living in the Trenches' and it was sung by the comedian in full kit with a blanket or pack, a French loaf, a couple of Mills bombs and a couple of candles

Blunden was briefly attached to the transport lines near Reninghelst. Whilst there he attended a concert party, which inspired his poem *Concert Party: Busseboom*. He tells of another performance at *The Fancies*:-

... better things were given us at the great hop-warehouse by the station, by our own divisional party, 'The Tivolies'. These oscillated round that well-known entertainer Du Calion, who perched on a ladder in the middle of the stage, wearing a pseudo-naval uniform, and let fall on the lordly brass-hats below his licensed satire beginning, "I should like to inform you young fellows of the junior service." Oh, then there was clowning, then there was

The Jocks of the 15th Division

the antic; Robinson, the tall immaculate in evening dress, danced with the tubby little 'wench', who snivelled to perfection, in lovely incongruity - what a roar went up when the 'wench' appeared again as a Lancashire lad of rather limited sense and confronted some tremendous stage colleague, with "Get out of 'ere". Or that other commonplace, fortune telling. The 'wench' was listening earnestly. The wizard read 'her' hand, scratching it. "Ah, there's a bit of luck for you. I can see it. There's the firing line. We don't 'ave no breastworks in this part. Ah, there's that bit of luck again. You're going to 'ave a letter. Your sweetheart's on the road to Poperinghe. He's been awarded the YMCA with Triangles. He's got off at the station. He's been told off by the RTO. He's gone in for a glass of stoot. He's come out again - they don't give credit. He's in the street outside. He's coming into this 'all. He's - (commotion at the back, shouting and blundering over forms; a red nosed gruesome figure, the like of which never rewarded Shakespeare's fancy, comes hurrying up the middle passage. Applause 'crescendo', all heads turned to the new Adonis) he's coming onto this platform!! (He does, and with one final tremendous gesture, glaring horribly at the gasping 'wench', flings out his scraggy arms in awful invitation. 'Alarums. Chambers go off'

This elementary but then glorious comedy was the last that some of the audience were ever to enjoy. But they had not expected even that much. One sees why they roared with laughter. Shakespeare died too soon.

Whilst billeted in Reninghelst, men of the 12th (Bermondsey) East Surrey Regiment recall it fondly:

When the battalion arrived the village boasted a YMCA, and an Expeditionary Force Canteen. Within a short space of time a Divisional Canteen, Supper Bar and Theatre had arisen next to the Divisional Headquarters. It was quite a treat to go into the supper bar and be served with a tasty dish by some of the neat Belgian girls who were employed there as waitresses. Prices were moderate, and the atmosphere was that of a restaurant in England. In the canteen English beer was sold, thereby taking away some of the custom from the few estaminets, including the "Swan," where the famous "Emma" dispensed hospitality. The theatre became the home of our well known Divisional concert party, the "Crumps," and some of the latest films from England were also shown there. The 'Crumps" party was formed of members of the 41st Division and had some notable *artistes* amongst them.

If anything, the Poperinghe area was better known by the troops for these divisional Concert Parties than any other form of entertainment. As professional as anything on offer in 'civvy street', the men who made up these troupes helped maintain the humour and morale of the soldiers who had to endure the horrors of the Ypres Salient.

A quiet evening playing cards

The majority of men in my battalion had given their cap and collar badges to the French ladies they had been walking out with, as souvenirs, and I expect in some cases had also left other souvenirs which would either be a blessing or a curse to the ladies concerned.
Private Frank Richards, Old Soldiers Never Die

5

GAMBLING & BROTHELS

WHEREVER THERE ARE large numbers of soldiers with money to spend, no matter how little, there will be a proportionate number of 'entrepreneurs' well-versed in the specialised art of quickly separating one from the other. Although strictly forbidden, gambling was rife in the camps. Everybody played cards, and many were the long nights spent in billets and cafés, under candle-light or shaded lights, with soldiers putting their pay-packets at risk. A favourite game of chance was Crown and Anchor, a kind of roulette where the only winner was the owner of the dice and the board. Those who gambled did so, for the most part, to stave-off boredom or to be sociable. Frank Richards wrote about his 'leisure hours' with his friend Duffy and their Corporal Pardoe:

During our leisure hours we played Kitty Nap, Pontoon, Brag and Crown and Anchor. A pukka old soldier's Bible was his pack of cards. Corporal Pardoe and I won quite a lot of money. Mine came in handy afterwards for having a good time, but Corporal Pardoe was thrifty with his winnings, and didn't spend hardly a penny. Duffy told me I was in God's pocket but that he had no doubt in his own mind that I would get killed during the next action I was in, and that all men who were lucky at gambling very soon had their lights put out.

Corporal Pardoe got killed. In a belt that Corporal Pardoe wore next to his skin they found about sixty English sovereigns, besides French money. None of it went back to his next of kin. I could have had some but I didn't want to touch it: I was satisfied with his puttees

Henry Williamson learned his lesson the hard way when:

... playing a strange and fascinating game called Crown and Anchor. The owner of the board called it 'Crown and Mud-'ook' - the 'lucky old mood-'ook'. He came from Yorkshire, where they do not weigh the anchor, but pull up the mud hook. Well do I remember that Mons hero's greeting of myself and friends when we walked into the estaminet and saw him sitting at a table surrounded by a dozen 'old sweats'. 'Well, boys, all welcome if you show the colour of your brass. They all coom 'ere with the seat out of their trousers, and go away in motor cars'. That man may have been a hero, but he was certainly a liar.

There was no point in trying to amass a fortune by gambling or saving; the soldier's philosophy was simple - spend it whilst you've got it because, next time over the top could be your last and if you get killed, either the enemy or your mates will get it anyway.

At Gwalia Farm in 1917, Colonel Rorie learnt a few points about gambling:

Here it was that we first had American M.O.s attached to the Field Ambulances and Battalions, and several of them remained with us to the end. The great majority turned out to be first-rate fellows, although a few had to get over the "effete Yurrup" stage before we took them to our bosoms: a week up the line was usually sufficient to adjust their outlook. But, in spite of little things like that, good chaps they were, and good comrades: their point of view was always fresh and stimulating; they gave us an outfit of terse and vigorous slang which some of us use yet; while the numerous new methods they shewed us of losing our spare cash at games of chance were both surprising and educative.

As well as the gambling there was the 'entertainment' that was frowned-on, though not forbidden by the military authorities. Extremely busy as they were during the day, the cafés, bars and estaminets of Poperinghe managed to provide a very active and lively offering of night life.

Rifleman W. Worrell, 12th Battalion The Rifle Brigade remembers well his time in the cafés:

We used to go into the Café des Alliés in Poperinghe. It was a popular place because there was a little man with a squeeze-box there and he knew all the right tunes to play. He'd start off with 'Mademoiselle from Armentières' but the universal favourite was 'The Monk of Great Renown', and sooner or later he got around to 'Aprés la Guerre Finis':

> Aprés la geurre finis
> Soldats Anglais partir
> Mademoiselle in the family way
> Aprés la geurre finis.

Sung to the tune of *Sous les ponts de Paris*, it needs no literal translation. Their is no doubt a great deal of intimacy did take place and undeniable evidence of it exists in the genealogy of many of the families in Poperinghe and its surrounding villages today. It was a standing joke after the war for the young men of Belgium, when jokingly questioning the parentage of friends, or having their own questioned, to plead ignorance of their true father, and quote their date of birth as being between 1914 and 1918.

56

In nearby Vieuxbec, one of the better-known places of questionable, if not forbidden, pleasure, was the *Estaminet de Réunion des Blanchisseuses*, run by a Madame Henriette Perret who was, according to Captain Philip Gosse of the Royal Army Medical Corps:

... a woman of generous proportions; her age, about forty. To assist her she employed two handmaidens 'Darkie,' that big, black-eyed, full-breasted romp of a girl, a great favourite with the British soldiers; and a fair delicately pale blonde, Berthe - pretty, with still a veneer of maidenly modesty which Darkie had lost long ago, if indeed she had ever possessed it. Madame Perret's most regular customer was a young sanitary corporal who had no fascination with medals or inclination to serve anywhere near the front. After completing his daily work he liked to spend as much of the remainder of the day as his money or Madame would allow, sitting in her estaminet sipping 'caffy-avec,' a mixture of coffee and chicory into which a little cognac has been added, and chatting, and even flirting a little with Darkie, or Berthe. Unfortunately, one day the corporal had one too many 'caffy-avecs' and, maddened by this poisonous mixture, he made violent love to Madame. Worse, the corporal so far forgot himself and the respect due to a lady of such dignity and position as to attempt to snatch the fruit without first shaking the bough. Madame's feelings were, naturally, outraged. After her 'ordeal' Madame was reliably informed by the local interpreter. Monsieur Junod. that: "all her neighbours were deeply shocked by the affair". In reality they all thought she deserved it and were not at all surprised. Playing on Madame's ego he continued: "Madame herself was famous for her good looks, and who could blame a young, a gallant and brave young man for falling violently in love with her? Some men, less particular, might have taken a fancy for Darkie, that bold hussy who tried all she could to attract the men, or that quiet, sly puss, Berthe. But no, the corporal took no notice of those two younger women, and had fallen in love with Madame". Junod told her how the corporal had confided "since first he saw her - he had been in love with the beautiful proprietress of the Estaminet de Réunion des Blanchisseuses, and how this smouldering passion had, alas overwhelmed his reason, with the dreadful result that the poor fellow, so brave, such a boy, must die a scoundrel's death". Madame's honour must be vindicated.

The question of honour was really a question of money, as, having spent all his money, the wayward corporal couldn't pay for Henriette's personal services. Secretly, she had been pleased with the the corporal's attention as, a few weeks later, the Town Major, Captain Scrivener, assigned him a permanent billet in the estaminet at Henriette's insistence.

Much of the female company did not come freely, and, from the day that Poperinghe became a garrison town, so there began a lucrative trade in prostitution; of which, it is questionably, but seriously, claimed "no

Poperinghe women took part; the majority of females the soldiers came into contact with were refugees from the surrounding region."

Most of the Poperinghe females who had chosen to remain in the town during the war either did so with their husbands and families, were self-sufficient, or managed to earn a living by selling souvenirs, running estaminets selling eggs and chips and cheap beer and wine, making and selling Flemish lace, and anything else that the thousands of soldiers were willing to buy. On the other hand, the female refugees were frequently forced to accept, and do, things they would never in normal circumstances have contemplated – and then there were those of course, both 'respectable' ladies of Poperinghe and the refugees alike, who were more than willing to earn a very good living doing what they knew best.

Bordellos and brothels were set-up in premises in and around the town – private houses, estaminets, restaurants, hotels, cellars, outhouses, and any other place that offered some privacy and the basic comforts:

> ... those cafés, half club, half brothel, which provided drink for the thirsty on the ground floor and solace for the bored upstairs.

As their fame spread, so did their number. Officially, there were two types of premises where prostitutes were allowed to conduct their business. A red light identified those passed as acceptable for NCOs and other ranks, and a blue light specified those thought suitable for officers. However, there soon flourished a number of other such premises showing no light or discrimination whatsoever, offering exactly the same service to any rank who wanted it, the only difference being the quality of the merchandise and the price. Edwin Vaughan inadvertently visited one of these on the road between Poperinghe and St. Jan-ter-Biezen on 30 July 1917:

> When we were a little way from Jan-ter-Biezen some evil genius prompted him to knock at the door of a dark, empty-looking house. The door was opened immediately and he was inside before I could stop him. I followed him and found we were in a kind of secret bar. Seated about were a sergeant, a police corporal, several privates with two or three girls and - horror of horrors - MacFarlane with his arm round a much-painted woman. Radcliffe struck an attitude and called to the stout woman behind the bar: 'Madame! Biere! Biere pour tous! Bags of Biere!'.

Many bordellos operated behind what appeared to be perfectly respectable facades, and others were active in what would be the last sort of place that the authorities would consider suitable. An account in the unpublished memoirs of Lieutenant Walter-Laing, dated 18 August 1917, entitled *Corps Laundry in the vicinity of Poperinghe* reads:

> At the end of the town towards Lovie Château was a large brewery, or works

of some kind, which had been turned into a Corps Laundry. Great numbers of Belgian girls worked here. No doubt most of them were refugees and lived in the shanties which these families had been able to erect along the roads in this neighbourhood. They were a chattering, laughing irresponsible crowd.

The Manageresses of these girls were two very good-looking women. One was quite young, and as far as I remember was known to everybody as Agnes. The other was older, but of much the same type. Agnes was a very clever girl, and retained her job in spite of much criticism. All the young officers thought she was charming, and some of the older ones thought so too! The counter-espionage people seemed to think she was a spy and investigated her affairs continually. Generals and head people thought she was dangerous in other ways, but she never seemed to get sacked. She had invented a uniform for herself, which was a cross between a nun and a nursing sister, and much more attractive than either; and both nuns and nurses petitioned the authorities against her wearing it, but without success. She undoubtedly had 'friends at court'.

Whilst we were in this area our Divisional Laundry officer was in charge of XIV Corps laundries and, as was usually the case, he was a man who could not be entrusted with the command of fighting troops, and yet was fit enough to remain on active service. He was an amiable individual called Ernest Platt, and was so thoroughly incompetent as a soldier that he was the joy of the Division - the exception that proves the rule! The more incompetent that Ernie showed himself to be, the more his many friends exerted themselves to find him pleasant and comfortable jobs. It was generally supposed that, early in the war, Ernie had been blown up by a shell which became the excuse for all of his many eccentricities. He had a bland smiling face, and his slightly watery eye indicated drink rather than shell-shock.

For some time now Ernie had been our Laundry Officer, and needless to say he found the job at Lovie simply ideal. On the Somme his sergeants controlled the private soldiers who did the work; but here, where we used refugee labour of a female gender, it was necessary to have female managers. Ernie's only concern, therefore, was to see that these manageresses were pretty and attractive.

Of course, Agnes managed him as well as the employees and Ernie was ideally happy. With his permission and support, she opened many new departments of laundry work, and employed great numbers of girls at the expense of the British Government. One of these departments was a place where officers' underclothing, shirts, socks etc.. were washed and mended, and large numbers of officers found it necessary to call and give them instructions for mending and washing by word of mouth. Ernie, in fact, spent most of his time in showing idle young officers 'round the factory', and Agnes was always near at hand to explain things.

I suppose it was more or less of a scandal really, but it provided much amusement to many over-strained fighting men during their short spells of rest from the Battle Zone.

In the British sectors, the number of bordellos and brothels was, as far as was practicable, strictly controlled by the Area Provost Marshal's office and regular checks, carried out to detect sexually transmitted diseases, were performed by the Royal Army Medical Corps.

Even Lord Kitchener, an old soldier of much experience, attempted to help with his seemingly pointless order of August 1914, a copy of which every soldier, not of his own doing, carried in his pay-book, stating:

Your duty cannot be done unless your health is sound. So keep constantly on your guard against any excesses. In this new experience you may find temptations both in wine and women. You must resist both temptations, and while treating all women with perfect courtesy, you should avoid any intimacy.

Sound health, in the soldier's opinion, had nothing to do with wine and women, or song come to that, and they felt that, what they should be warned to be on guard against, was bombs, barbed wire, shells, bullets, damp trenches, lack of food, itching lice and aggressive Germans. As for "you should avoid any intimacy", it would hardly have been given a thought when the opportunity arose to avoid some of it.

It was small wonder, in a world of madness, where both soldiers and civilians were constantly reminded of their own mortality, that the intimacy between man and woman, culminating in sexual release, was often nothing more than the end of a mutual search for comfort and sanity.

Henry Williamson, seemed sympathetic to this:

'Fife,' said Madame in her fat double-chinned voice. 'Fife' and she held up five fingers. 'Champagne,' he said recklessly and gave her three five franc notes. She smiled, 'Now spik to Suzanne. She spik English. Quite clean girl. She make you much happiness.' Suzanne waved to him, he entered closing the door behind him. She looked up and smiled and he tried to overcome his disgust as she spat on the floor. 'Don't be shy, old soldier,' she said. 'No' he said, waiting. 'Poor bloody Tommee,' she said, smiling at him indirectly. 'This bloody war no bloody good, eh?' He began to feel a little bit better and even dared to caress the top of her head. She grabbed his hand, put one of his fingers in her mouth and, pulling him down on the bench next to her, she began fumbling with him. Then came the booze. He had a few glasses and began to convince himself, while trying to haul her heavy body onto his knees, that he was beginning to feel the way he should be feeling.

Ridding his non-masculine shame he turned rough and she gave him a clip about the ears, yelling at him with a strong menacing voice, a mixture of Flemish and French, from which he ducked away like from a machine-gun in the middle of night in no man's land. She told him to go to hell, the 'bastard, dirty English asshole' etc. Then she saw his eyes and, putting her arms around his neck, she pressed her mouth firmly to his as she pulled him down on the bench.

The inexperienced and the young were easy prey for the ladies of the night, and in the early part of the war the venereal disease rate was very high, and the study of protection, prophylactics and treatment took on a new emphasis. In Poperinghe, although prostitution was tolerated, the occasional prostitute would be arrested by the Military Police and subjected to an examination by the medical authorities for evidence of any sexually transmittable disease. Women found to have a disease of this nature were reported to the Area Provost Marshal's office and their places of work designated out-of-bounds. A memorandum between the Belgian Provost department and the Area Provost Marshal's office in Poperinghe, regarding two 'illegal' prostitutes, dated 2 June 1918, details:

Further to your query of 7th May I have the honour to inform you of the resultant conversation between myself and Dr. Dewulf, doctor attached to Health and Hygiene Services, at this address. The named Madame Lucie and the girl Julia, residing at Villa Steenstaete, on the road between Proven and Poperinghe, were found after presenting themselves for examination, to be displaying none of the clinical symptoms associated with venereal disease.

Many accounts have been written of the queues of men waiting their turn outside various establishments, and many of the prostitutes, and certainly their 'Madames,' were said to have made enough money from the services they sold to set themselves up in shops and restaurants, or to become café owners and hotel proprietors in the post-war years.

There was no doubt that 'scarlet ladies', or any ladies come to that, were actively sought by men of the British Army. During the course of the war syphilis and gonorrhea in all British sectors were responsible for more than 15,000 soldiers being constantly out of action. A soldier's proficiency pay was stopped for the time he spent in hospital as a result of venereal disease, and home leave stopped for a period of twelve-months after leaving the hospital. As it was, no man in his right mind would want to take this extremely difficult-to-explain souvenir home to his wife or sweetheart. Unfortunately all this carried little weight, as statistics at the war's end showed 20 hospitals with 11,000 beds in the UK, and 9,000 in France, were devoted solely to venereal disease cases.

Poperinghe under Shell Fire, 19 December, 1915. A sketch by Wilfred R. Wood, Artist's Rifles

Around the Flemish-School picture made by the towers and gables of the town, a great cloud of brick-dust bellied out, while in measure with it rose a clamour of shrieks, falling masonry, footsteps and scatteration. It was our baptism of fire.
Lieutenant R. H. Mottram

6

BOMBS & BOMBARDMENTS

P OPERINGHE WAS FIRST BOMBED whilst occupied by the French when a British 'plane accidentally dropped one on the Cheese Market in Pottestraat. Luckily no one was injured, although a number of windows were broken by the blast. Two days later a German aircraft dropped a bomb in the Mesenstraat, close to the town square, causing a number of casualties. Throughout the war the destruction caused by aerial activity was great, both in terms of damage and casualties, amongst civilians and military alike. With its large concentration of British troops, Poperinghe became a regular target for night bombing raids and shelling by long range guns, although the town was fairly safe from shellfire until the shortening of the Salient in 1915 and the Battle of the Lys in 1918. Captain Hugh Pollard remembered being shelled in Poperinghe:

The Brigade had detrained at Hazebrouck, marched from there to Poperinghe, and spent the night in billets and hutments. Soon after dawn 'Whistling Rufus,' a long range 5.9 German naval gun that came up on a railroad truck, opened up his morning hymn of hate from some distant point on the Ypres-Menin railroad within the German lines. The shells screamed through the air to fall about the scattered straggling streets of Poperinghe; some fell without bursting, burying themselves in the soft ground of the gardens in the rear of the houses, others burst in a high column of black smoke and the dull rumbling collapse of brick and masonry. The long streets and the Grand' Place were practically empty except for a military policeman or so taking what cover was afforded by the narrow doorways. The shop fronts were closed with scarred and splintered boarding where once there had been glass windows, but 'Pop' had been within range since April 1915. A covered motor ambulance with the Red Cross on its sides tears hastily up the street, round a corner, and speeds on to where a shell had caused casualties in a billet. The whole town seems to crouch together, everybody is motionless and silent while the bombardment lasts.

"Salute from the Salient" says the veteran sergeant; "nothing but a little morning strafe. Wait till you are past the Menin gate for shells - my word!"

The firing is at regular intervals - then it ceases as suddenly as it began. A weary subaltern has been checking it by his wristwatch. He waits till two periods have gone by. "Think it's over now, Sergeant. Fall the men in"

By the early spring of 1915 enemy bombing raids had become a regular feature of daily life, especially on market day when large crowds gathered on the market square, as was the case on 12 March 1915. At 2.25 pm there was a raid during which a number of bombs were dropped by German 'planes. Two landed on the corner of the square and Veurnestraat, a few yards from the house of J. Notredame (now housing the Bank Générale) killing 11, wounding 25, and smashing many windows. At 4.30 pm on the same day, a second raid took place during which two large bombs were dropped, one landing by the church on the Abeele road completely destroying two motor-ambulances and the windows of a headquarter mess. The other, which fortunately did not explode, falling on a brewery beside a line of lorries. Three days later the streets were lined with onlookers when military-style funerals, attended by high-ranking British, Belgian and French officers, were given to the victims of these raids – five townspeople, three refugees, two Belgian and one English soldier. Photographs of the carnage caused were widely distributed to the people of Poperinghe as a propaganda campaign aimed at maintaining the dislike of anything German.

Sometime during the shelling, tragedy struck the family of Jeanne Batheau:

At the beginning of the war my little sister Rachel was two and a half years old. One of my aunts had fled to Normandy and wrote regularly to my parents asking them to send us to stay with her, but my parents always refused. One day Rachel was in bed, fast asleep. Suddenly my father came running into the room and shouted "Get Rachel out of her bed, we'll get bombed!" My mother ran to the child but she was too late. Our house almost got a direct hit from a bomb. There was a big explosion which smashed the window, spreading glass everywhere. My mother and Rachel were caught by the blast and covered with glass. Rachel was in a state of shock and paralysed with fear. She used to be such a lively child, beautiful black hair, always talking – how she changed after that. She completely lost her appetite. Not far from our house there was a hospital where my parents were told there was a very good doctor. They took Rachel to see him and he examined her. After a while he turned to my parents and told them "You must spoil her - this little girl will only live until she is 5 years old." He was right in his prediction, Rachel died in 1917 - she was 5. When she died her hair was white and she had become blind and dumb. During her final two years my sisters and I transported Rachel everywhere in an old pram. A few days after Rachel was buried my mother wanted to visit her little grave, This turned out to be impossible - a bombardment had destroyed that part of the cemetery - Rachel died twice.

The hospital Jeanne Batheau mentioned was where today's Poperinghe Old Military Cemetery stands.

On 22 April the Germans launched an attack using asphyxiating gas for the first time in the Ypres Salient. The French line opposite Brielen was broken, causing widespread panic among the defending troops. As far back as Poperinghe, units were ordered to stand to arms, and all vehicles undergoing repair had to be made mobile as soon as possible. Practically the whole of Ypres was in flames, a sight easily visible from the church towers in Poperinghe. The following day there were large movements of British cavalry and infantry through the town on their way to what was now desperate fighting at the front. Streams of motor ambulances passed through the streets, hospitals rapidly filled to overflowing, and bell tents were pitched to cope with the increasing numbers of the arriving wounded. Throughout that night a terrific bombardment raged all along the front, and its effects soon began to be felt in the back areas, with the smell of gas wafting through the streets. Civilians were advised to keep all their doors and windows tightly closed and shuttered in case of the gas itself reached the town. When the smell of gas had dispersed, and the danger of its arrival negated, they witnessed large numbers of Canadian wounded being brought through the town. With the hospitals unable to cope, these men were laid out on the town square to receive whatever attention could be given there. Jeanne Batheau remembers:

It happened so unexpectedly. Suddenly a lot of lorries came down the road we lived in loaded with French and British soldiers. British officers ordered us to go with them. "Come on girls, come on!" We had to carry buckets of milk and try to give it to the gassed soldiers. It is just impossible to describe what they looked like. Poor men, they ripped off their clothes in agony, their eyes goggled, they were spitting out their lungs. I still hear them shouting and crying - I will never forget that – and we were so young. A lot of people don't realise Poperinghe was not a safe town to live in, of course, Ypres was completely destroyed during the war, but Poperinghe was heavily shelled and bombed regularly. My mother's niece was staying with us, she had a little boy 18 months old, they were the victims of another gas attack. The little boy lived to be 28 years old. So many lives were destroyed by gas.

British Cavalry officer Frederick Coleman arrived in Poperinghe on 24 April shortly after the town had received its first bombardment by the enemy's long range guns:

We entered Poperinghe at the gallop, and were surprised to find the inhabitants running around in great fear and confusion. A very frightened Belgian told us six large shells, fired from far behind the enemy line, had landed in the town just a few minutes previously.

An officer, publishing a section of his diary in the Toc H Journal after the war, signing himself only as 'H.A.T.', witnessing the above bombardment first-hand, had noted:

At 7.30 on April 24th Poperinghe received its first shelling which lasted about an hour and a half. The kitchen of the officers' mess to which I was attached was blown to bits, one soldier killed and the other four or five in the room all wounded - two severely. My batman and my small hound, 'Peter', were luckily not in the mess at the moment. 'Peter' met his death a few weeks later under the wheels of a Belgian car. One of the Corps Intelligence Officers put this epitaph over his grave:-

> O, Bishop leave this grave unbless'd,
> For here lies Peter now at rest -
> No Christian but a little dog,
> Run over by a Belgian hog.

On the morning of the 25th German 'planes flew over the town and, instead of dropping bombs, gave smoke signals, the meaning of which we were soon to learn. At 2.30pm Poperinghe was shelled for some time - shells arriving at regular intervals of ten minutes, but luckily some were duds. This shelling was carried out by a German railway-mounted gun which moved from time to time to pay its attention to other parts of the line, until it was eventually put out of action by us. The chief casualties that afternoon occurred among the nuns in a convent close to Corps HQ.

On April 26th, 12 inch shells began to arrive in Poperinghe at 4.10 pm, and some big explosions occurred. The first one dropped only a few yards from Corps HQ. Orders for the move of HQ, already contemplated, were issued and we were on the move by 6 pm. Darkness was coming on, and there was much congestion on the road leading to Abeele, the site of our new Headquarters. Besides military transport there was a vast quantity of civilian traffic as the people evacuated the town. Straggling families and their slow-moving carts helped to block the way, for it must be remembered that our traffic control had not yet become as efficient as it was later to be. It took many of our heavy lorries three or four hours to travel a distance of as many miles to Abeele. There were, as always on such occasions, many pathetic sights and many requests from Belgians for lifts on our already overloaded transport. This evacuation of Poperinghe by V Corps HQ was, of course, quite a minor event. It was made because Abeele was then out of shelling range and the work of HQ could thus escape interruption, and also in the hope of saving Poperinghe greater damage.

The first 12-inch shell to land in Poperinghe scored a direct hit on No. 68 Pottestraat; a large crater, and a pile of rubble, were the only indications that the house of Emile and Jeremie Warrein had ever existed.

Once occupying a prime position on the market square, the estaminet *A la Maison de Ville* suffered considerable bomb damage on 2 July 1915, and again on 4 October. Forced to close, its facade provided a convenient site for bill-posting and was finally demolished after the war to make way for. the town's war memorial. Its immediate neighbour, *A La Fontaine* at No. 8 on the square still stands, although it is now known as café *Du Tram*. Behind *A la Fontaine* was a small café - *t'Kapitteltje* - which was completely destroyed by a direct hit. The butcher's shop of Jeremie and Louise Muyllaert-Meneboo and the *Hotel de Grand Cerf*, immediately opposite, were both destroyed simultaneously. The local newspaper, *'t Nieuwsblad*

A La Maison de Ville estaminet, used as a poster-site after it was damaged by bombing

van Poperinghe, ceased printing when Eugene Willem's book-store and print-works (now the Hotel Amfora) was shelled. Alfons Diericks-Ramoen, the organist of St. Bertin's Church, lived next door to Eugene, but his house, remained untouched. By 1918 the *St. Stanislas Academy of Art* at No. 17, Vlamingstraat (now the Pol de Rynck), where typhus inoculations had been carried out in 1915, was destroyed along with all the neighbouring properties up to the house of August Devos-Vandromme, the blacksmith, at No. 23 (now 't Wiegje). Also destroyed were the cafés *In den Hert* and *Au Faisan Doré* in Veurnestraat, *In de Hesp, Au Chasseur*, and *In de Landing* in Bruggestraat, *In de Nieuwe Wereld* and the popular *In 't Katje* in Casselstraat, *A la Ville de Dunkerque* on the corner of Duinkerkestraat, *De Valke* in Baljuwstraat, *A St. Omer* in Burg Bertenplein and the local brewery, *Brouwerij Six-Colpaert*, in Reninghelstplein. A house used to billet 50 men was totally destroyed, but luckily empty at the time. The Municipal Cemetery suffered bomb damage resulting in the destruction of many graves and the forced exhumation of numerous corpses The church of St. Bertin suffered superficial damage on 5 May 1915. Heavy shelling caused considerable damage to the church of St. Vedas, while completely destroying the streets and houses nearby. The local Benedictine nuns were evacuated after their convent was shelled on 13 and 21 May, and, just a few yards away, the Convent Pauline suffered superficial shrapnel damage.

As early as 8 August 1914, at the suggestion of the town's Burgomaster, the owner of a nearby château on the road to Proven, Baron Mazeman de Couthove, had given permission for it to be used as a hospital. A bombing raid on 25 April 1915, caused damage to the château and resulted in the death of four nuns and six patients who were suffering from typhus. On a visit there Geoffrey Winthrop-Young wrote:

Down again at Poperinghe, I found that the civilian hospital had just been shelled, in which we had sent some of our sick, and they began to take in wounded British soldiers at the Sacré Coeur. Four nuns were killed and twelve old women, many wounded. I fetched cars and cleared them out, a dreadful business, in a panic of the staff. The old people half dead already with terror.

On 20 January 1916, the French newspaper, *L'Echo de Paris* reported:

Poperinghe, like Veurne or Nancy, is within range of the German field-guns. Despite the real danger which they are under, a large part of the population does not wish to leave the town, and continues to live there. Since the beginning of the war, 37 civilians, including three children and sixteen women were killed there. Amongst them, nineteen were victims of bombs dropped by German airmen. Likewise, 29 soldiers were killed.

A few weeks later General Ponsonby, Commanding Officer of the 2nd Coldstream Guards, noted in his diary:

March 3rd 1916. This afternoon we came in for some shelling. The Germans started shelling the town about 1 o'clock. One shell pitched into a neighbouring house killing 6 men of the Durham Light Infantry and wounding a lot more. Our verandah got broken up a bit, several shells came into the Grand Square causing a bit of panic and the inhabitants began scuttling down their cellars. But the bombardment soon fizzled out and we were able to have our luncheon in peace. The shells were not big ones, rather a new type that makes a swishing sound as they pass over, probably fired from some long range naval gun.

March 4th. Shelling started again about 8pm. causing alarm and consternation in the dark, but as far as I can gather very little damage.

The damaged Municipal Cemetery

Shelling commenced again after we had gone to bed about 1am. The proprietor and his wife rushed into Roger's bedroom to beg him to retire to their cellar, but he stuck to his bed and the noise came to an end about 2am. These midnight visits from explosives are beginning to be most unpleasant.

In 1917, Royal Field Artillery Signaller, Aubrey Wade, looking for a hot beverage in Poperinghe, met a woman in a house near the railway station who touched him deeply when he started talking to her about her husband and children:

Next to the road there was this detached house with a small garden in front of it. I went down there knowing that in every house in Belgium you will be offered a cup of coffee. The door was wide open and when I knocked on the door a woman of about 40 years old, grey hair, looking a little weary, came out of a side room "Café?" "Oui, madame, s'll vous plait." It was ready in a second and there I was, sitting in her barely furnished kitchen, talking to her in stumbling French. Was she not frightened here on this road to Vlamertinghe, so close to the front? Did her husband join the army? She glanced at a picture of a soldier on the wall. Ha! Henry was a corporal. "Kids Madame?" I asked. Yes she had children - Two. "At home? Here?" "In the garden, m'sieu" she explained. I stood up to look at them, wondering what possessed her to keep children so near the front at Ypres, but I couldn't see anyone in the garden, nobody at all. But she insisted, "Of course, m'sieu, there they are, you see!" And I did. In the shadow of a low hedge stood two small crosses, next to each other, decorated with flowers.

Poperinghe was the last stop on the Hazebrouck–Ypres railway line and the better part of troops and equipment that came to the town did so by rail, arriving at Poperinghe Station. During the course of the war countless thousands of men passed through the town from here. Consequently it became a favourite target of the German long range guns, in particular the one salvaged from the battleship Admiral Tirpitz which, sited 25 kilometres away, was permanently aimed at the station. Arriving infantry would frequently experience their baptism of fire here. In his book *The Wet Flanders Plain*, Henry Williamson gives his account of trains arriving in Poperinghe:

The troop trains arriving at "Pop" by day used to behave peculiarly as they approached the station through the acres of hospital hutments and military cemeteries. Card parties squatting on the wooden floors of the trucks were liable to be thrown forwards, jerked upright, and flung backwards. Cling! –clang! –plonk! –plink! –crank! ran from buffer to buffer along the grey length of the train. Then another jerk, the frantic puffing of an engine whose wheels were racing on the rails, and the train went on, faster and faster, rattling through the station, and stopping half-a-mile past it. Then perhaps

A near miss for the church

we might hear a noise filling the air as though the sky were a dome of solid glass, and an immense diamond were cutting a slow curve down it. A hard noise, as of gem-hard dust being ground away. As it drew nearer it changed to a coarse vibration of steel, opening a furrow in the very heavens, droning, buzzing, hissing, dropping in scale to a deep bass and growing louder and louder, a noise enormous and terrifying; and then a geyser of black smoke and wooden sleepers and stones arose, a rending metallic *cra–ash*, a great deep smoking crater under rails twisted and blue-scaled with heat, the whining zip of hot splinters, and the thudding down of lumps of wood and earth. A seventeen-inch howitzer shell, fired from a dozen miles away, from behind one of those ridges the taking of which "cost" (in the language of all-dominating property) nearly half a million casualties in 1917.

In the spring of 1917, Second-Lieutenant Bernard Martin, 10th North Staffordshire Regiment, arrived at the station with a draft of reinforcements:

The train to Poperinghe stopped just in front of the station. A panorama of chaos revealed itself before my frightened eyes - a derailed train with wagons fallen into a huge shell-hole in the road, a large signal tower reduced to a pile of splintered wood from which some twisted remnants of mechanical parts stuck out. Station buildings with large holes in the walls and roofs, broken glass everywhere. This first encounter with the damage caused by war shocked me. In my imagery of war men fought against each other with guns, bayonets and revolvers, somehow I had never thought of the material damages or, perhaps, my imagination had not extended that far. I once saw slums and old ruins being demolished with a pick axe in England but never any modern building or new mechanical construction maliciously destroyed - pure barbarism!

Edwin Vaughan, arrived there with his regiment during a bombardment in the early hours of 29 July 1917:

Crash! Crash! Crash! and something ripped through the roof of the carriage and smashed a window. In the pale light of dawn I saw Edgerton... "What was that?" I asked. "Shells or bombs," he replied. "We must be somewhere near Ypres."... as we climbed down onto the deserted siding, a dishevelled RTO hurried along the train. "Poperinghe" he said in reply to our enquiries. "There's a guide waiting for you on the road; get away as soon as you like, they have been shelling us all night." Nothing loath, we hurried our troops on to the cobbled road and marched away before any more shells fell.

Later in the day Vaughan and a friend were exploring the town:

Along the Ypres road, opposite the station, we found the Officers' Club - a most inviting and comfortable place with a verandah in front where we lounged in deck chairs and drank whisky whilst watching the chains of vehicles crawling past towards Ypres. The station opposite we eyed askance, for it was very near and the buildings were almost entirely demolished by shellfire, while the much worn rails were surrounded by shell-holes and debris.

The following day, contemplating dinner at the Officers' Club (now café Falstaff), he experienced much more than a pleasant meal:

I got a drink, carried it onto the verandah and had just sat down when there was a whizz and a crash as a high velocity shell burst in the garden behind. I beat it into the dining room as a dozen more arrived. The fact that two hit the house next door and brought half our ceiling down speeded the departure of most of the drinkers. When all was quiet I went out again with another fellow and resumed my seat on the verandah.

A train at this moment drew up in the station and we smiled to each other as, on the sound of a whistle, a detachment of brand new artillery men tumbled smartly out and ranged themselves 'in fours facing the train' according to the drill book. They had just received the command 'Right' when a shell landed smack in the middle of them and we turned sick to see a fountain of dust, smoke, bricks, khaki and equipment spurt up from the panic stricken column. Great confusion followed, men running away from the scene, wounded men struggling into the club or dropping on the road, officers dragging wildly at the reeking contorted bodies and a stream of shells pitching into or around the station.

There were 16 dead and many wounded all of whom were quickly despatched in ambulances, while the remainder of the scared tyros were marched off to camp.

The Welsh Guards, on preparing to leave the area in 1917, were to experience:

... that night, commencing at 7 p.m., there was a most determined and extensive bombing of the whole area – Siege Camp, Vlamertinghe, Elverdinghe, Dirty Bucket Camp, Caestre, Poperinghe, the Switch Road, all got it in the neck; the performance going on without intermission for five hours to the accompaniment of continuous crashes. At one time there were seven 'planes caught in the searchlights – four of them right over our heads – and the noise of the "Archies" and machine-guns, added to that of the bomb explosions, made up a chorus sufficiently diabolical to stick in the memory. A steady stream of casualties poured into the Dressing Station.

By midnight there were only a few 'planes left, chiefly "returning empties" making for their own lines again; and at one a.m. the unit fell in – with a 'plane again plumb above us, golden in the searchlight's beam – and marched to Proven, preceded an hour before by the transport who had gone through a stiff time, both before they left Siege Camp – where a dud bomb landed beside them – and on the road. the route to Proven – twelve kilometres – was simply stinking with explosive products from the numerous bomb holes on it and beside it; but only an odd bomb or two fell en route, as the night show was practically over; and we got to the station at our scheduled time (3.50 a.m.) to entrain after a cold two hours' wait on the platform.

At 12.30 am, 22/23 March 1918, several shells landed close to Talbot House at No. 35 Gasthuisstraat. Tubby Clayton, lying half awake in his bed was interrupted in his musings by his servant bursting in and exclaiming "There's a woman screaming somewhere and I can't a-bear it!" He then rushed down the stairs and out the front door, followed shortly by Clayton himself. Across the street a smoking pile of bricks and rubble was all that remained of Cyrille's Restaurant (now Muzikwinkel Delbaere); an Officers' Only establishment run by Cyrille Vermeulen and his wife Leonià Tanghe. Searching the wreckage was Clayton's servant and cook. One survivor, a man wearing only a shirt, on asking Tubby for help, was given the padré's pyjama trousers. Returning to Talbot House, Clayton sent his carpenter to provide whatever assistance he could whilst he hurried to the Officers' Club and fetched a fire ladder. He then went to the Town Hall, to ask Captain Strachan, the Area Provost Marshal, for aid. Returning to Gasthuisstraat he found the Town Major and his staff had turned out to help. Of the eleven people on the premises at the time, only three came out alive. The decapitated body of Cyrille himself was found almost immediately, but it was not until later that his head was discovered in a shop across the street. Also killed were the Vermeulen's four maids, two sets of sisters Madeleine and Maria Leclerq, and Germaine and Maria Vanhove.

In 1930, having spent the war attached to the YMCA, Barclay Baron felt that Poperinghe may not have been the safest place to be, but it was a refuge from the relentless misery of trench warfare and the boredom of the camps. His summing up of Poperinghe from 1915 – 1918 read:

All these scenes – bombing, shelling, evacuation, troops and supplies moving up, wounded coming down - were for the next three years to be the familiar portion of life in and around Poperinghe. Geography had made it a funnel through which Division after Division was poured into the Salient and returned, battered but unbeaten out of it. The town remained (with a few dangerous interludes) the first strictly habitable and homely place for the man coming out of the Ypres fighting. Its houses grew shabby with the marks of shrapnel, and a few were completely destroyed, but by comparison with life a few miles eastward, it seemed wonderfully safe. The streets were full of life, the shops were open, the women cooked countless omelettes for soldiers, the children went to school. Beer and barrel organ music were purveyed by its estaminets, pictures by its improvised cinemas, it was a warm and friendly place, and men counted it good fortune to be there.

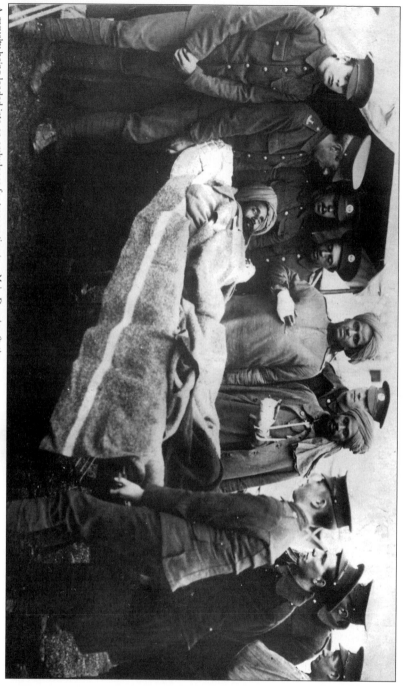

A casualty being loaded into an ambulance for transporting to a Main Dressing Station

I'm on my way to Mendinghem
With a ticket home to Blighty
Why did they send us over here
Oh Jesus Christ Almighty.
Lester Simpson

7

CASUALTIES & CARE

B Y NOVEMBER 1914 an epidemic of abdominal typhoid had broken out
amongst the citizenry of Poperinghe, coinciding with the huge
influx of refugees and the arrival of the French army. Padré van
Walleghem in writing of the outbreak recorded:

December 1st 1914, Tuesday. Due to the overcrowding, the negligence of
the soldiers, and perhaps numerous other reasons, a widely spread illness
known as diarrhoea developed in this region. Some suffer only slightly but
for the elderly, and the sick, the illness is life threatening. Few days will pass,
from now on, without me having to administer the last rites. There are dead
horses lying everywhere which the French refuse to bury, this does not
improve the conditions.

Shortly thereafter the Burgomaster ordered the population to be
inoculated against typhus. By 2/3 February 1915, a systematic programme
of vaccination was in full swing as the population, which by this time
consisted mainly of refugees, were inoculated against the disease. Initiated,
financed, and staffed by the Quakers, the St. John's Society and the Friends
Ambulance Unit, they supported and assisted the civilian and medical
authorities throughout the back areas. All non-combatants, they were
ultimately responsible to Geoffery Winthrop-Young the Poperinghe area
Friends Ambulance Unit Commandant. Throughout the winter of 1914-15
his staff provided invaluable assistance, organising search parties to ensure
everybody was vaccinated and segregating those who were infected. The
houses of those found to be infected were marked with a 'V' and - when
the civilian hospitals overflowed - quarantine in the Château Elizabeth on
the outskirts of the town. The typhus bacteria was found in the drinking
water and the local beer.

Following the shelling of Poperinghe on 25 April 1915, the town
hospital, and an annex in the Château Elizabeth, were evacuated and
transferred, by invitation, to Château Couthove, the home of Baron
Mazeman, where they continued their work in large purpose-built barracks

in the Château grounds. Padré van Walleghem, visiting the hospital, wrote:

I thought the wards looked very healthy and was informed the wounded are taken good care of. Reverend Callewaert was chaplain, he is an assistant padré of Saint Martin's, Ypres.

Primarily used to care for Belgian soldiers and civilians the hospital was staffed by ladies of l'Aide Civile et Militaire Belge. British VAD Alison MacFie served here in 1917 recalling:

The Hospital Elizabeth was situated in a field behind Château Couthove a few kilometres from Poperinghe... a side line of the Hospital was the keeping going of the lace making industry. The Lace Car used to go out every day, taking the thread to the skilled lace makers who remained in the area, and collecting their work when finished.

The weaponry used during the war caused the opposing armies enormous casualties on a scale unlike anything before. Existing medical procedures had to be completely re-evaluated and, by mid-1917 the Royal Army Medical Corps had devised an efficient system of hospitalisation and care extending from the front line trenches, right back to the hospitals on the French coast, and onward to similar establishments throughout England. A casualty could be evacuated from the front line through a series

Quakers in khaki

78

of strategically positioned aid posts where his condition would be assessed and treated accordingly. Firstly he would be taken to the Regimental Aid Post, manned by a regimental Medical Officer and a senior Royal Army Medical Corps NCO near the support lines. His condition would be assessed, his wound recorded, and a label with the relevant detail affixed to his uniform. If his wound did not impair mobility, and was deemed to be of a non-serious nature, he would be classified as Walking Wounded and despatched, unaided to a Collecting Post for further evacuation. Stretcher cases were removed directly to the nearest Advanced Dressing Station, staffed by a Royal Army Medical Corps Captain and orderlies, normally sited behind the front lines in a suitable building or custom-built underground concrete shelter. Here the casualty would be thoroughly examined, the exact nature of his wounds specified and, in emergency cases, surgery would be performed. These aid stations were usually near to a Collecting Post and Field Ambulance Unit from where, after treatment and processing, the wounded could be evacuated to a Main Dressing Station.

Commanded by a Royal Army Medical Corps Major, up to three miles behind the Advanced Dressing Station, the Main Dressing Stations were established in a large complex of huts and tents where the treatment of wounds began in earnest. Those with minor wounds were attended to and

Walking Wounded at a Collecting Post

Stretcher cases and Walking Wounded awaiting attention at an Advanced Dressing Station

Collecting Posts for the Walking Wounded took many forms

despatched to a Divisional Rest Station. The more seriously wounded would be operated on, if necessary, and kept under observation for a minimum of 24-hours, or until such time as they were stable enough to be transferred to a Casualty Clearing Station.

Gwalia Farm Hospital, the farthest Main Dressing Station from the front, was a short distance outside of Poperinghe on the road to Elverdinghe. Sited alongside the Peselhoek–Poperinghe–Woesten rail junction, it was surrounded by Browne Nos. 1, 2, and 3 army camps and the St. John's supply dump. Opened in late June 1917, the first casualties to be treated at Gwalia were from the Battle of Messines. By 31 July 1917, it was the Main Dressing Station of XIV Corps with their RAMC personnel quartered in Browne No. 3. From early September until November 1917, heavy shelling forced the site to be temporarily evacuated.

The large barn at Gwalia Farm was the receiving room, where all arriving casualties were entered-in the Admission and Discharge Book, given anti-tetanus serum, and sorted out. From there, moribund cases and cases unfit for removal were taken to a hospital Nissen hut; those fit to be fed taken to a feeding tent; those requiring immediate attention to a surgical dressing room; those who were gassed to special tents where oxygen apparatus, etc was kept. When dressings were done the casualties were

An International Walking Wounded get-together

Unloading the wounded at a Main Dressing Station

The Hospital Tents at Gwalia Farm

taken to a row of large hospital tents, again fed if necessary, and looked after till the Motor Ambulance Convoys took them back to the various Casualty Clearing Stations. This was the responsibility of Dispatching N.C.O.s: head cases and chest cases going to one Casualty Clearing Station, fractured thighs to another, gas cases to a third, general cases to a fourth, and so on.

Field Hospitals, made up of Casualty Clearing Stations, which were much larger versions of the Main Dressing Stations, were to be found anywhere between 8 and 15 miles from the front. Each Station was commanded by a Royal Army Medical Corps Lieutenant-Colonel with a staff of specialist surgeons, physicians and nurses. Here, those who were badly wounded would receive urgent attention and surgery.

Prior to the opening of the 1917 summer offensive, the British Fifth Army medical authorities, foreseeing the possibility of large numbers of casualties, raised the number of Field Hospital complexes from 11 to 15. Anticipating up to 20,000 casualties on the first day – the capacity of each was increased from under 300 to over 1200 beds.

Situated at Brandhoek, a small village sitting alongside the Hazebrouck–Poperinghe–Ypres railway line, on the main road from Poperinghe to Ypres, was the Brandhoek Medical Aid Station, supported by a Field Ambulance based in the village's school buildings. Opened in mid-1915, by 1917 it had become Brandhoek Field Hospital, comprising Nos. 32 and 44 Casualty Clearing Stations and No. 3 Australian Casualty Clearing Station, it was the nearest of its type to the front line. Due to the high risk of infection from septicaemia and gangrene, specialised abdominal, chest and thigh wound operations were performed here, together with amputations and the removal of shell fragments and the like. A local recalled the surrounding area being continuously littered with dead and dying men:

After the bombardment they arrived in dozens loaded in ambulances or sometimes in railway wagons. They were simply dropped outside until they were dead, then my brother and I searched their pockets before they were buried. We were only four and five years old. We were inseparable until one day my brother lagged behind when the shelling started. He sheltered beneath the bench in the guards' cabin and escaped unharmed. Shortly afterwards, nevertheless, he died from the shock that raid caused him.

On 26 July 1917, the complex at Brandhoek was in a state of preparedness for the 31st July offensive. Dr Harvey Cushing remembers:

After lunch a young captain from Brandhoek legged it in. They have put up their advanced CCS during the past five days, and are ready to 'take in' tomorrow - being halfway between Poperinghe and Ypres, shells go over their heads both ways. If the coming push does not result in an advance in the first few hours they will be heavily bombarded. No.44 and the 3rd Australian are not as yet set up, but soon will be. He says there are thirteen teams at No.32 - doctors and nurses have been pouring in for the past few days.

And two days later:

No. 32. is ready for work, though the sisters haven't come up as yet. Colonel Sutcliffe, a big bodied soul, was tramping about in the mud fixing up his final duckboards. There are nine teams of abdominal surgeons ready for work. No.44 is less ready, but still far enough along. The 3rd Australian also was floundering in the mud and getting established...These three CCS's are necessarily alongside both road and railway, for hospitals and ammunition dumps must compete for sites of the same kind - hence they are likely to be heavily shelled, but this afternoon was comparatively quiet.

A few hundred yards away, at Red Farm on the Brandhoek crossroads, No. 46 Field Ambulance, 15th Division, was commanded by Lieutenant-Colonel Arthur Martin-Leake, VC and Bar; the first man to be awarded the Victoria Cross twice.

At work in a Dressing Station

On 31 July 1917, he recorded:

The first cases arrived at 5.10 this morning. Other cars were sent up at once. The first car from the Menin Road arrived two hours later. Clearing (of casualties) has been satisfactory except on the Potijze side, especially during the afternoon up to about 8pm. The difficulty was caused by the amount of traffic on the Potijze road. The cars took a very long time to get up and down this portion of the route. The accumulation of cases at one time reached about 40 but I don't think it passed this figure. The posts were cleared by 10 pm completely. A good many stretcher cases were carried to the Prison by Germans and cleared from there by car. A good many walking cases found their way to the Prison and char-a-bancs were sent for them. Here work has gone smoothly and there has never been any great accumulation. We have had 4 Medical Officers working. No dressings have been changed unless there was some special reason, and cases sent on to CCS with as little delay as possible.

During that day alone, 2,153 casualties were recorded as passing through No 46 Field Ambulance. 48-hours later one of the staff, a Dr Colston, recorded the meeting of Lieutenant-Colonel Martin-Leake with Captain Chavasse, VC:

A Hospital train about to leave a railhead at a Casualty Clearing Station

2nd August. An Ambulance came up tonight and in it was Captain Chavasse, VC, RAMC, of the King's Liverpool Battalions of the 55th Division. His face was unrecognisable, all blackened from a shell-burst very near and he seemed to be unconscious. As he had an abdominal wound besides I did not take him out of the Ambulance which was sent on direct to 32 CCS where he will probably die.

Chavasse died two days later, posthumously awarded a Bar to his Victoria Cross.

By 21 August heavy shelling was making life at Brandhoek intolerable. Martin-Leake noted:

About 11 am today shelling began in this neighbourhood. Two shells fell in our area close to the building. There were lots of patients about at the time but nobody was hurt; this is to be accounted for by the wet and soft ground where the shells pitched. Shells have dropped in the three CCS, and Number 44 has had a nurse and orderly killed. The shelling has continued on and off all day, mostly near the Railway. CCS evacuated in the evening.

The Brandhoek site was abandoned by 25 August, due to the incessant bombardments, and the Casualty Clearing Stations relocated to Lijssenthoek.

Hospital tents at Reninghelst

Sited beside the railway sidings on the Hazebrouck–Poperinghe railway, between the premises of local farmer, Remy Quaghebur, and the road to Boeschepe, just outside the range of the enemy's guns, the hospital complex at Lijssenthoek began in mid-October 1914 as the French 15éme Hôpital d'Evacuation. From late June 1915 until the Armistice the site, known as Remy Sidings, taking its name from the railhead and Remy Quaghebur's farm alongside it, was occupied by a succession of British Field Hospitals – Casualty Clearing Stations Nos. 10 & 17 from July 1915 to April 1918; No. 13 from August to September 1917; Nos. 32, 44 & 3rd Australian from August to November 1917; No. 62 in the latter part of 1918, with No. 10 Stationary Hospital still operating there in November 1919.

Padré van Walleghem, visiting here in 1916, wrote:

August 22nd, Tuesday. Between the inns 'De Leene' and 'De Booenaert' I walked along the Boeschepe Road through the great beautiful hospital of the British. What large tents! There are many big tents standing in a field that has been turned into a park with shrubs, flowers, lawns and lovely little trees; just like the children's colonies in Wulveringhem. The hospital covers several acres and a whole army of doctors, nurses and stretcher bearers are employed here.

In late 1917, Remy Sidings had a capacity of 4,000 beds. Considered to be too close to the front during the 1918 spring offensive, the complex was moved further toward the rear area. It was replaced by a number of British and French Field Ambulance Units until the Casualty Clearing Station was set up there again toward the end of the year.

As a medical orderly, Walter Sutherland, 3rd Canadian Casualty Clearing Station, tended the wounded at Remy Sidings. In 1998 his son George, writing of his father's experiences, said:

They brought the men here from the fighting front. Hundreds of horse-drawn carts, loaded with the wounded and the dead, were brought over the cobblestones. The blood was dripping out of the wounded - the wounded soldiers - and then they were brought into the hospital. That's where my father had the job of selection - some of them to be taken into the hospital, some of them to the mortuary. On one occasion my father took what he thought was a dead person into the mortuary and he heard a groan, he looked, the chap was still alive, and he took him into the hospital where they saved his life.

Most casualties arrived at Remy Sidings by ambulance and, if necessary, were evacuated immediately by hospital train to one of the Base Hospitals at Boulogne, Etaples, Wimereux, Hardelot, Camiers or Le Treport. Those too seriously wounded to be cared for at these hospitals were shipped to England for treatment.

Slightly to the north, between Poperinghe and Krombeke, the Casualty Clearing Stations at Westvleteren – Nos. 4, 47, 61, 62 and 63 specialised in the treatment of wounds caused by unidentified types of gases. There was also a separate section for contagious illnesses and a guarded area where men with self-inflicted wounds were located. Originally commanded by a Colonel Chopping, the name Choppinghem was suggested for the site but changed to Dosinghem or Dozinghem to suggest a less brutal form of care. According to soldiers who knew Dozinghem, it was an easy target. When British gunfire hit one of the enemy hospitals near Roeselare or Menin, retaliatory fire was sure to follow. It was never proved that the enemy deliberately fired on hospitals, but Dozinghem was regularly shelled and bombed despite its large, electrically lit, Red Cross sign.

Between Proven and Roesbrugge, Casualty Clearing Stations Nos. 12, 46, 61, staffed mostly by personnel from Philadelphia, U.S.A., and No. 64 Casualty Clearing Stations, dealt with head wounds and those caused by chlorine gas. On 12 July 1917, 100 gas cases were being dealt with at station No. 46 with a capacity of 200 beds. In preparation for the Passchendaele offensive it expanded this capacity to 1,300.

The first gas cases came to this Dressing Station on the Poperinghe Road

The Germans first used mustard gas in large amounts on the night of 13–14 July 1917 causing 3,000 casualties. A second gas attack a week later caused another 4,000. Dr Harvey Cushing, attached to the Mendinghem Field Hospital in 1917, attending a lecture, on the properties of this latest weapon recorded in his journal on 18 July:

A characteristic oedema of the larynx and conjunctivae, which comes on late, and, most striking of all, the remarkable cutaneous manifestations with great patches of purple pigmentation, which seem to come out wherever there has been any external pressure, as from a belt. Apparently the gas is comparatively odourless and sent over in shells, the symptoms do not appear until after quite an interval.

Five days later he was well acquainted:

Poor devils, I've seen too many of them since - new ones - their eyes bandaged, led along by a man with a string, while they try to keep to the duckboards. Some of the after effects are as extraordinary as they are horrible - the sloughing of the genitals for example. They had about twenty casualties out of the first 1,000 cases, chiefly from bronchial troubles. Fortunately vision does not appear to be often lost.

The dressing station today

On 2nd August he noted:

Pouring cats and dogs all day - also pouring cold and shivering wounded, covered with mud and blood. The pre-operation room is still crowded - one can't possibly keep up with them; and the unsystematic way things are run drives one frantic. The greatest battle of history is floundering up to its middle in a morass, and the guns have sunk even deeper than that. Operating from 8.30 am one day till 2 am the next, standing in a pair of rubber boots and periodically full of tea as a stimulant, is not healthy. It's an awful business, probably the worst possible training in surgery for a young man, and ruinous for the carefully acquired technique of an oldster. Something over 2,000 wounded have passed, so far, through this one CCS. There are fifteen similar stations behind the battle front. 10.30 pm. We're about through now with this particular episode. Around 30,000 casualties, I believe.

The patient-counter for recording the number of those treated at No 46 Casualty Clearing Station was reset to zero on 21 September after 20,000 men had been admitted and treated, but it didn't stop there, the workload continued unabated.

Amidst the suffering and death surrounding Harvey Cushing and his staff, there were some moments of respite. Invited to attend tea with the Scots Guards at nearby Privet Camp on 11 August, he had scarcely arrived when:

... sounds of bag-pipes came in out of the rain, and a person who stands six feet six appeared - a pipe major. He almost filled the little stone-floored room - his longest pipe a few inches from the beams of the ceiling - and what little of the room he left was filled with his music... at the end I was presented with a glass of whiskey - full - of whiskey - which I had to give to Mr. Pipe Major - very seriously... the concert was given for me... I politely asked him for another and he blew up his bellows and gave what they said was a 'Skye Boating Song' - very mournful... A pouring rain outside.. .this big kilted giant... the World's Champion Piper.. .a strange situation for me, even in this summer of strange situations.

This complex of Casualty Clearing Stations was going to be called Endinghem, but this was thought as being a little too close to the mark, even for the the hard-bitten troops to cope with, and it was decided to change the name to Mendinghem. The Mendinghem Stations were still in constant use throughout most of 1918.

During Third Ypres, Nos. 62 and 63 Casualty Clearing Stations were sited at Haringhe. No. 62 Clearing Station was specifically set up to deal with NYDN (Not Yet Diagnosed Nervous) and psychiatric cases. For the most part these were the victims of concussion, shell-shock, battle fatigue and PTSD (Post Traumatic Stress Disorder). Neuroses and cases of psychotic anxiety had begun to manifest themselves very early in the war but few cases were identified and treated. Despite evidence to the contrary, High Command remained adamant in their opinion that the fighting soldier would not be psychologically affected by his experiences. Although a great many men were psychologically affected, inexperienced Medical Officers failed to identify the symptoms, seeing the men concerned as either 'shirking', 'windy', 'suffering from funk', or just plain 'cowardly'. Gradually these opinions were dismissed and the Staff forced to recognise that battle neuroses was a very real problem. In the majority of cases, prolonged bombardments and the conditions experienced at the front were listed as the cause of this condition, soon classified as 'shell shock', and it was assumed that removal of the sufferer from the cause would effect the cure. By the summer of 1917 sufferers continued to be treated with extreme suspicion. Far removed from the front, it was hoped that those who found their way to Bandagehem would, after a period of one month's evaluation and care, be either 'cured' and returned to active duty immediately, or evacuated to a base hospital. In keeping with the other two major field hospitals, Haringe was suitably nicknamed Bandagehem.

Dr Cushing, not at all impressed by those at Bandagehem, said:

Bandagehem I find is misnamed. They don't bandage at all. A walk over there along the tracks to tea at No. 62, where all the NYDN cases are congregated, in other words shell-shock cases - very dismal! A dumping ground for MO's who can't wriggle out - none of them appear at all interested in, or acquainted with, psychiatry.

Walter-Laing, when referring to Bandagehem, Mendinghem and Dozinghem, noted that:

Only the Doctors appeared to be allowed to walk out with the nurses; although sometimes they used to come and listen to our Band performances, and then other officers got a chance of making themselves agreeable to them. These nurses spent their lives either in the Wards or in hutments caged in with barbed wire entanglements for all the world like a lot of German prisoners, and their opportunities of amusement appeared to be few. They were real workers however, and they were subjected to the nightly bombing raids just the same as other people. So they had a hard time and we respected them for it.

The names Dozinghem, Mendinghem and Bandagehem given to these Casualty Clearing Stations were well-suited to the humour of the British troops and became part of their vocabulary. As with 'Blighty', these three were part of their parlance when referring to accidental injuries, bomb or shellfire wounds and battlefield casualties.

A bivouac camp in a Flanders field

I've a Little Wet Home in a Trench
Where the rainstorms continually drench;
There's the sky overhead,
Clay or mud for a bed,
And a stone we use for a bench.
Private Michael Riley

8

CAMPS & DUMPS

BILLETING THE VAST NUMBER of troops supporting the infantry, as well as the infantry itself, caused a major headache for the authorities. Some of the 'luckier' troops found billets in nearby houses, cottages or farm buildings, but Poperinghe itself could not cope with housing all of its new military population and consequently developed a sprawling suburbia of military camps embracing and linking a multitude of its surrounding hamlets and villages. Vast camps of tents and huts were set up in the back areas to billet men during their stay in the region. The tents were draughty and invariably leaked whilst the huts, with leaking roofs and no glass in the windows, were little better. Nevertheless, they were akin to luxury for the troops compared to their life when in the trenches.

Annexes to the Remy Sidings Casualty Clearing Stations at Lijssenthoek saw further camps of tents and hutments stretch for miles along the access roads. With such names as Peerless, North and South Atlantic, Zealand, Waratah, Moonta, Scrabo, Mud Farm and the like, they provided billeting for medical staff and divisional troops When the Canadian Expeditionary Force arrived in early 1915, the Town Major of Poperinghe was forced to create a separate sector in which to billet them. Between April 1915 and June 1916, their 1st and 3rd Divisions were billeted in and around Reninghelst in camps named Ontario, Quebec and Ottawa. The arrangement was later extended to include Australian and New Zealand troops who had their own camps - Auckland, Wellington and Pacific. By 1917 a string of Canadian camps stretching between Reninghelst and Vlamertinghe named Toronto, St. Lawrence, Erie, Winnipeg, Montreal, Halifax, Vancouver and Moose Jaw were added to this relatively small area. Others in the area were the 6th London Regiment's Scottish Camp, the 7th London Regiment's Dominion Camp, "famed for its large rat population", and the Devonshires, Downshire, and Red Horse Shoe Camps which housed in excess of 150,000 men.

There were also numerous artillery batteries situated hereabouts;

A Canadian camp at Abeele

Working on Belgian farms had its advantages

sheltered behind the Scherpenberg, where their muzzle flares could not be seen. Nevertheless, they were the continuous target of night-time enemy bombing raids.

On 2 April 1915, an agreement between the Allied armies and the Belgian government entitled civilian owners of premises used by the army to claim payment.

Integrating the army with the civilian population usually proved mutually beneficial. Units billeted in farms would invariably find part of their duties involved working with the harvest. Belgian farmers would have preferred to use Belgian soldiers, but these were only given access to British sectors by necessity. "Which is why," wrote Padré van Walleghem "farmers who accepted British soldiers were by far the better off. Although the job was only half done, it was at least half done."

Captain James Dunn, R.A.M.C, Medical Officer to the 2nd Battalion, Royal Welch Fusiliers, speaking of his farm billet, was to say:

> Our landlady told me that her potatoes were very good until the heavy rains. 'C'est la guerre,' she added. She's a buxom decent soul; we have pumped her cellar dry for her. The cottages are gaily painted in vivid blues, greens, red and yellow, within and without: doors, window frames and cornice are generally white. There is nothing of the scented air and unsightliness of the French midden, but, in a very porous soil with a high ground-water level, the nearness of the open cottage well to the cottage privy is gruesome. The flea and the gnat outnumber the louse in the billets here.

Ouderdom and its hamlet Zevecoten, just southeast of Poperinghe, was to become known as 'Little London', a home from home, with canteens, supper bar, restaurants, and a YMCA hut. It was used primarily as a rest area for troops, Field Ambulance units, horse-lines and a centre for both divisional and brigade headquarters. Captain Milne of the Leicestershires was pleasantly surprised when he and his battalion moved into his new billet here:

> ... the battalion marched through the warm summer night to Ouderdom, a hamlet a few miles from Poperinghe, where by midnight it was bivouaced in an open field. There it remained for a week, resting, route marching, bayonet fighting. It was flooded out by the torrential rain of a heavy thunderstorm, but it dried itself and was as cheerful as ever.

> It was a pleasant bivouac. There was a farmhouse with its usual supplies of café au lait; there was a homely-looking windmill; there were one or two cows and a very young bull in a field; there was also "Les Trois Amis," an estaminet, where hock was supplied in a little back garden where one sat on a rickety chair by a tin-topped table and the daughter of the house (a rather plain girl) wearing a black dress and black cotton stockings came to

and fro with the glasses.

It was warm summer weather and for a week it was not a bad war, even though shells dropped on our horse lines a hundred yards in rear, which caused the woman at the farmhouse to go first into tears, then into hysterics and finally into the cellar.

Not everyone was so happy. Surgical Specialist Arthur A. Martin, describing his billet at Ouderdom in his book *A Surgeon in Khaki,* wrote:

Our Ambulance headquarters was about the most God-forsaken place that one could possibly imagine. The first impression one received was a dirty pond, full of fetid water and surrounded by heaped-up straw manure.

Closely abutting this putrefactive manure was the cottage itself, with one front room, a kitchen a rickety stair led up to a windy loft full of corn and hops and bags of potatoes. Twelve medical officers, two chaplains, and a quartermaster lived in the tiny little front room, or crowded round a table in it. Six or seven officers slept on the floor of this den at night. The O.C. and Chaplain slept in the box off our only room and the rest of us slept in the loft amidst the wheat and hops and the bitter cold draughts.

We met many Flemish besides Madame and her family at this time, and

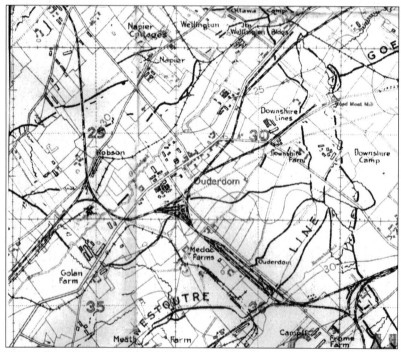

Section of a trench map showing Ouderdom and its surrounding camps

although we sympathised greatly with them, we could not bring ourselves to like them. It was all so different with the French, whom we liked and who liked us. The Flemings did not seem to care for us; they certainly never made us any demonstrations of affection. Perhaps it was the difference in tongue. They spoke French with an Irish-Dutch brogue, and our accent was, of course, a pure Anglo Saxon.

Tommy Atkins as a rule likes everyone, but he neither understood nor cared for the Flemings. This was quite noticeable. We found those round Ouderdom, Ypres, and Dickebusch sullen, dour, and suspicious. We were not welcomed, and their surly, heavy manner towards us was very apparent. There was no responsiveness, no *gaieté de coeur,* no cheerfulness.

Nor was Lieutenant-Colonel the Hon. R. G. A Hamilton overjoyed with his lot. In his diaries, later published under the title, *The War Diaries of The Master of Belhaven,* he made it quite clear how he felt about things:

To-day I have been quite busy as I had to go round the ten farms occupied by the squadron and pay the weekly bills for forage, etc. It is rather a business, as I have to make out all the bills myself in triplicate, and argue it all out with the farmers' wives. Their husbands are all away fighting, but they

Surgical Specialist Arthur A. Martin outside his billet at Ouderdom

97

know exactly how many centimes there are in a franc. In fact, they are as bad as natives at bargaining. Most of the people round here are very willing to help us, but some of them are brutes.

They are not really French but Flemish, though most of them speak French fairly well. I am depressed beyond words at being back in this vile country: I hate the Belgians and Belgium. We are billeted in a filthy farm, full of squealing children, and dirty beyond words. It is like all the farms in Flanders, only a little worse.

The usual depressing Belgian weather: mud and dirt everywhere. The people of the farm are, of course, pro-German. I have no doubt they would betray us if they got half a chance. I have warned everyone that they must now consider themselves as in a hostile country.

This farm has more flies to the square inch than other place I have yet met; it is also dirtier and children more noisy. Altogether, a more offensive place could not have been found for a rest camp in all Europe.

We are suffering from a plague of flies here: they are an absolute pest. Fortunately, we have a good supply of fly-papers, and these become black with flies as soon as they are put up. It is horribly insanitary as all the flies come straight off the enormous manure-heap that fills the yard of every Flemish farm. It is almost sarcastic to call such a filthy place a "rest camp." However, we are away from the incessant roar of the guns for a time, which

A YMCA hut alongside a light railway

is certainly a blessing.

After a lot of trouble with our landlord - who, like all Belgian-Flemish farmers, is hostile to the English - we moved off and marched south into France at Abeele. We have got distinctly better billets this time, except there seems to be no means of making a fire in our room, and it is horribly cold on the stone floor.

To-night we are in the same farm as we had coming out of action six weeks ago. The room with seven doors, all letting draughts—and the horrible family who walked through the room from 4 a.m. onwards at one-minute intervals. It is one of the worst billets we have had out here.

His opinion hadn't changed much when, after serving for a time in France, he returned:

.... and crossed the Franco-Belgian frontier at midday. Once more I am back in this hateful country! My wagon-lines are about a mile and a half from Poperinghe on the Ypres side. Never have I seen such a filthy place to camp. The battery who were here before me (D/80 of the 17th' Division) must be quite the dirtiest lot in the Army. I do not complain of the mud, which is in many places up to the horses' girths, but of the filth and refuse left round the men's sleeping quarters. There is only a small farm with two rooms, so that it is quite impossible for the officers to live there. We have a big house in Poperinghe itself, close to the cathedral.

An officer in the 1st Battalion Welsh Guards had his own opinion of Belgium too:

On March 15th a move was made to a camp in A.30 Wood on the other side, north-east, of Poperinghe. This was a much better camp. All the men were in good huts built in a wood - and there were excellent baths. The officers' baths, by the way, were apparently given by the Empress Club.

The whole country-side was alive with men, and here and there a monster gun stuck its ugly snout out of a wood or the side of a harmless-looking house. Altogether it was the busiest part of the British line. A constant stream of traffic went up and down the road, men on foot, men on horses, carts, waggons, motor-cars and lorries. Aeroplanes in numbers were buzzing round when the weather was decent - captive balloons appeared as steady black dots in the sky.

There were a lot of civilians who used to wander about - dirty-looking people who spoke a kind of pidgin English, and lived by selling chocolates and apples to the men.

In peace time no one would wish their worst enemy in Poperinghe - in war time, for those in the salient, it was the hub of the universe. It is a vile little town in the centre of a vile district.

All round Poperinghe were camps - their name is legion - but we are only concerned with those at St. Jan ter Biezen, where there were two together, one in the wood north-east of the town, A.30, and one on the road to Ypres not far from Vlamertinghe. In any of these camps the battalion was said to be at Poperinghe.

At one time or another most of the British army had been in this area. All have stories of Poperinghe - "The Fancies," "Ginger's Restaurant," and so on.

Infantry officer, Lieutenant F. C. Curry noted in his diary in 1915:

It was rather a wretched day we spent in this little farm. Heavy rain had turned the orchard in which we lay into a bog, and all the straw we could beg, borrow, or steal from inhabitants could not keep us out of the mud. Here too found the first instance of friction between the troops and civilian population and the old lady at the farm made no bones about telling us how unwelcome we were. She opened hostilities by taking the rod from her pump so that we could not fill our watercart, and the troops retaliated by stealing bundles of unthreshed wheat. This was speedily put a stop to (and paid for) by the officers, and for a while – peace reigned whilst she did a growing trade with cups of coffee and glasses of weak beer. Then one day, some of the officers saw some fresh baked bread in a little room off the kitchen, and offered to buy some. To our surprise, the old dear started to wave a knife around dangerously and screamed at us: "You take my wheat, you take my water, and now you won't even leave me my bread. I would rather the Germans were here... at least they pay for what they take". As we had just paid for all her straw we thought that a bit thick, and pointed out if the Germans were here, we would fear for her safety and that of her two slatternly daughters doing a roaring trade with the coffee and beer among the troops thronging the farm. This at least quietened the old lady and she saw our point!

There were those who accepted things as they were, before changing them to suit themselves. One such man was Lieutenant-Colonel Seton Huchison, Commanding Officer, 33rd Battalion Machine Gun Corps. Its time at Boone Camp, sited in fields between Abeele and Poperinghe, is described in the battalion history as:

Boone Camp our Rear Echelon, our home from home, for four busy months. At the outset the C.O. prepared a comprehensive scheme for Camp construction, based on a definite system of salvage from the battle area, by means of light railways and horse transport. The object of laying out the Camp was to provide a pleasant Camp for the entertainment of the Minimum Reserve, all Companies being in the line, and the Reserve being changed every two weeks. Shops, in neat, tiled huts, with red tiled sloping roofs were first made, followed by Officers' Messes, the Headquarters Mess being designed in four separate buildings, all under a camouflaged verandah; a splendid Canteen and three Recreation Rooms, with an Open

Air Beer Garden, shaded with camouflage net erected above it. A Hospital with twelve beds; a Church with a richly carved oak altar, salvaged in Vlamertinghe, and Brass Vases and Ornaments made from shell cases by the Artificers, whilst imitation Stained Glass Windows were painted by Private Arthurs on sheets of oil cotton, and placed in the windows.

The Transport Lines were particularly fine and organised by Captain L. R. Hutchison, the twin brother of the C.O., who was now posted to the Battalion. Besides standings, harness rooms, forage barns, farrier's shop and sick lines were constructed, with a twenty foot well sunk, providing 300 gallons of water per diem for watering.

Daily runs at 6.30 a.m. for one and a half miles were the order of the day, and owing to these, the splendid balmy weather, the vigorous inter-section football matches and those of basket ball, a new American game, and the excellent menu system organised by the Quartermaster and R.Q.M.S. Scott, the health of the Battalion improved daily; so much so that when the "Spanish Flu" had gripped the Division, together with the rest of the civilised and uncivilised world, we survived with half a dozen mild cases.

Boone Camp, a fine boon to all, was an athletic and scholastic paradise. Much too soon we had to leave it and bid our adieux. We wonder who now inhabits its enclosure and violates its Transport Lines, where vicious mules

Part of Lieutenant-Colonel Hutchison's Boone Camp

ate the trees and kicked their drivers. No runners now dash out from its precincts for their early morning run; no Scouts for a bathe in the forbidden pool, defying wire and willows; no footballs seek refuge in that little central pond where the blue caddie fly dances. Sports, boxing, the Shrapnels, the band, barrage drill and other amusements with which the happy summer hours of 1918, on our rest days were beguiled, are things of the past. Perhaps its tiles and timbers are now displayed in many a Watou shop; new green grass may now have obliterated our wanton tracks – yet its site will still remain – a little sloping meadow, a little pond with willows near the bottom, a small hedge surrounding, studded closely with lofty elms and poplars, two of which, scarred and dead, decorated by the shreds of a fallen aeroplane, will tell for a little time of the war that once did wage.

By early 1916 Hoograaf and Busseboom, on the outskirts of Poperinghe, were surrounded by horse-lines and camps. When the 47th (London) Division moved into Hooggraff, they too found a way of making their camp acceptable, describing it as:

... a dull and depressing slice of country, almost dead flat, intersected by beeks and ditches, with a few somewhat squalid clusters of houses at intervals, and covered with frequent hut-camps that required incessant labour to keep them drained and habitable. As time progressed these grew

Horse-lines formed part of the profusion of dumps, camps and hospital facilities in the back areas

and multiplied, together with new railways, heavy and light, dumps, horse lines, heavy battery positions, "sausage" balloon stations, and all the impediments of the war of position. An excellent arrangement was that units coming out of the line always went to the same camp, and thus came to regard it as theirs, taking more pride in its upkeep and amenities generally than if they had been only casual occupants.

Regardless of the opinions of those units entering Belgium, the Army was dependent on the cooperation of the local community. Farmland, hopfields, barns and outhouses were commissioned for camps and billets, farm-tools and equipment were used by the troops - frequently damaged and often never returned. Gates, fences and sheds were 'salvaged' for a multitude of uses, and hop-poles 'disappeared', only to re-appear, as dugouts, corduroy roads. trench cladding and, of course, firewood. Supporting this military need, Captain Dunn was to record:

Keen frost and bitter cold. The men have been burning gates, farm utensils, latrine seats, any combustible for a little warmth. Hop-poles were especially favoured, some were more like telegraph poles; to pinch and get away with them was an art.

In 1916, Lieutenant R. H. Mottram was billeted in the Benedictine Convent:

We were billeted in a deserted convent. I have since tried to recapture the sensation of sleeping on the stone floor of a nun's cell, and waking in the morning to see the blue smoke of our cookers rise against the last gloriously russet leaves of a great chestnut tree in the garden. The first night there was neither whisky, wine nor beer but someone procured a bottle of Creme de Cacao and we drank that and water.

Captain Dunn and his Royal Welch Fusiliers were billeted in the same premises during the Christmas period of 1917. He said of it:

The whole Battalion is in a convent, with a blown in gable, off the Rue de Cassel, but Pop makes any employment tolerable and any billet acceptable. This billet is just accepted. Its spaciousness, shoddiness, and the bareness of the rooms aggravate the effects of chilling currents from large broken windows and ill fitting or ever-open doors, of tiny fireplaces and, at first, lamentably little fuel: thanks to the diversion of a wagon of coal we no longer perish. The town is a sight. There is a daily movement of troops through it, a lot of troops are billeted in it. The whole atmosphere has been Christmassy for days; nothing so like the Christmas-tide at home has been seen out here. Christmas shopping is in full swing. One sees that there are no women and children, and scarcely misses them. All the shops, and there are lots of them, are full of goods and buyers, and doing a roaring trade.

A little to the east of Ouderdom, in the vicinity of Downshire Lines, a signpost reading 'This Way To The War' indicated towards Voormezeele and

Burgomaster Farm at Dickebusch

Troops resting in camp at Dickebusch

the front line at Vierstraat, St. Eloi and Hill 60. Somewhat further along this road, near Downshire Camp, stood the windmill, *Goed Moet Molen* and another signpost 'Confusion Corner'. In 1916 a road was constructed across the fields, starting at *Goed Moet Molen*, to link up with the network of narrow farm tracks and minor roads that criss-crossed the region. To the northwest, it led to the Vlamertinghe road and the string of Canadian camps eastward, in the southeast it ran, via Downshire Camp, to St. Hubertushoek and the camps Micmac, Surrey and Warburg. The troops found this corner very confusing, hence its nickname. In August 1917 Trooper H. L. Hall attempted, unsuccessfully, to dodge a fatigue party whilst at Micmac Camp:

> We had not been long settled down in this camp when the rumour spread that a fatigue party was wanted for a particularly nasty job, in or close to the front line; just what the job was nobody wanted to know from experience, so most of us being by now seasoned soldiers and experts at 'dodging the column' the camp was soon deserted.
>
> I was not quite sure of things, so I secreted myself in the camp and watched points. Sure enough, men were being lined up, but it was obvious from the sergeant-major's voice, manner and vocabulary, that the party was not large enough.
>
> Other tactics were then employed which proved successful. A voice boomed out, 'Come on boys, roll up for your cigarette issue,' and so the greener members of the community were caught, for this was a call not to be resisted. I chuckled to myself as the party numbered off and, when I was confident that I was safe, I casually made my way into the open. But somehow my luck seemed to have deserted me for a while, for when I came into view I was spotted and greeted with a shout from the sergeant-major of 'Hi! you come on, we want just one more man here, and you know the ropes; get on the end of the file.' I was caught, but my wildest dreams of rotten fatigues did not come near to the nightmare that this job was to be.

Between 1915 and 1917 one of the largest concentrations of troops, transports and horse lines, in the salient were sited in and around the village of Dickebusch. Built behind Melon Copse on the farm of Marcel Coene, the first camp here, Dickebusch Huts, was much favoured by the troops. Other camps followed – Walker, Canal Reserve, Albermarle, Smyth, Pioneer, Burgomaster Farm, Dickebusch West and New Dickebusch. By early 1917 the Dickebusch Huts, having become "rat infested and lousy beyond description", had lost their attraction and were turned into an ammunition dump which was destroyed on 27 May 1917.

Following Second Ypres, Dickebusch Huts gained notoriety when, over a period of 40 days, the British Army executed 8 men on, or near, the camp. According to van Walleghem the comrades of these men made a show of

105

visiting the graves "possibly in silent protest of the injustice".

Dickebusch was constantly shelled and:

> There was no safety anywhere in the accursed salient, even for troops resting out of action, such places as Dickebusch were no sanctuary. 'C' Battery, of the 2nd City of Edinburgh Brigade, had pulled out of the line, moving with all prudence; had crossed the dangerous spots of the Lille Road, and the Cafe Belge, swinging safely at last into the wagon lines west of Dickebusch. The horses had barely been watered, fed, and made ready for the night, when a shell landed at the end of the lines. The men were turned out and stood to the horses, taking them off the line and ready to move off. Another shell fell in the next field; the horses, trembling and sweating, fidgeted about. An anxious ten minutes passed, and then with an awful crash another shell fell. Right in the midst of the men and horses it burst with the reek and fumes of high explosive. As the dust cleared away it revealed a horrid calamity; 9 men and a number of horses were killed outright and a great many wounded by that one shell. The centre sector no longer existed.

Approximately two and a half miles northwest of Dickebusch was a complex of three farms called *Drie Groens*. In 1917 a segregational camp was built here to house labour battalions of the British West Indies Regiment. Achiel van Walleghem had experienced very little of foreign nationals prior to 1914, and West Indians were the subject of much curiosity:

> Saturday, May 26th 1917. At Drie Groens niggers arrived from Jamaica, in the West Indies, to work hereabouts. Dressed like all British soldiers, they are both civilised and softly spoken. Generally, however, they are not very popular because they have long fingers and civilians, in particular, would much rather see them leave than arrive. Whenever they enter a house for a coffee they might stay all afternoon or for just five minutes. I came across a letter to one of these black people from his mother; what Christian and motherly feelings she expressed, not one of our mothers express herself better. Extremely frightened by the shelling, these black people stare afraid when they hear a shell approaching and, when it hits the ground nearby, they dash off as if possessed.'

On 27 May a bombardment killed four British West Indies soldiers, wounding three others. At Gwalia Farm, after a West Indian Labour Corps camp was badly bombed, the scene in the dressing-room was described by Colonel David Rorie, D.S.O., T.D., M.D., D.P.H., in his *A Medico's Luck in the Great War*, as:

> ... the place was suddenly filled up with wounded niggers. Naturally emotional, and, equally, scared to death, besides – in many cases – being

badly injured, the black men made the dressing-room an inferno of shreaks, groans and cries which it was impossible to still. "Hallelujahs" broke out sporadically in various places; one man started a Moody and Sankey hymn, the chorus being taken up in fits and starts by others till a rival tune from another corner bore it down... as one gazed around the dim-lit hall of suffering at the gleaming teeth and rolling white eye-balls of the recumbent blacks on the operating tables and stretchers, the scene and din, inside and outside, suggested an impromptu revival meeting in nether regions...

Colonel David Rorie said of his billets at Gwalia Farm:

This was a land of hops and hop-poles. Our mess was in the tile-floored kitchen of a little farmhouse whose owners lived in the back premises – father, mother, grandmother, two young children and three adult male relatives, one of whom was killed during our stay by a shell which landed in a field on the other side of the road. The kitchen had a wide and high fireplace recess in which was fixed a stove. This kitchen was the dining and sitting room accommodation for the officers of the three Field Ambulances supplying personnel for the Corps Main Dressing Station: our sleeping quarters being Armstrong huts – none too weather-proof – and tentage in the neighbouring field.

There was only one small shallow dug-out of sorts available on our site; for the deep – and safe – dug-out was an impossibility, as water was usually struck at a depth of five or six feet or even less. All one could do, therefore, against shell or bomb, was to sandbag the huts and tents to a depth of three

Hospital tent at Gwalia Farm

An Army Service Corps dump on the outskirts of Poperinghe

Light railways networked the areas to meet all the supply demands of a modern army

feet or thereby, and trust to luck that no direct hit occurred. In some cases the ground on which a tent was erected was excavated for two or three feet and the tent sunk in it; while some of the more cautious hut dwellers had a trench dug in the floor, in which, should the spirit so move them, they could uncomfortably and moistly recline when Jerry was soaring skywards.

I have already said this was a land of hops and hop poles. It was also a land of spies and rumours thereof. One method said to be employed was signalling by smoke from house chimneys - bunches of wet straw being put on the fire at intervals as per code. The location of our tanks in a wood was said to have been thus given away, with resulting destructive attention from bombers; and it was also said that the spy, caught later in flagrante delicto, was obliterated in the mud by an appropriate and lucky tank accident. How many spy yarns there were throughout the campaign! windmills and church clocks worked to catch the balloonist's eye; men following the harmless, necessary plough and women laying out their innocent white washing, all according to plan for the edification of the watchful enemy flying man. True enough these stories were in many cases: the Boche was – and is – a methodical and wily animal: and those who deliberately choose to forget it are the sons of folly.

Until May 1915 the village of Proven, between Poperinghe and Roesbrugge, was used to billet French troops. After Second Ypres British troops were quartered in the village and the French took over Roesbrugge. A busy rail-head, a many-branched network of railway lines centred here and, because it was considered to be relatively safe from enemy shelling, its environs were used extensively for the storage of supplies and ammunition dumps. The village itself billeted troops, with thousands of men of the Army Service Corps and Chinese Labour Gangs camped in its neighbourhood.

East of Poperinghe, on either side of the Elverdinghe road, were spread a profusion of camps - Oakhanger, Ryde, Browne 1, 2 and 3, used by members of the Royal Army Medical Corps – as well as storage depots, horse-lines, gun batteries, hospital facilities and ammunition dumps. With gun batteries sited throughout, the area was the constant target of enemy guns. A light railway across the region ran from Poperinghe via Oosthoek, and Peselhoek via Dromore Corner, joining together near Alexandra Farm before halting on the western outskirts of Elverdinghe. A large ammunition dump, situated where the railways joined, was destroyed by a bombardment in 1917.

Serving with the 2nd/5th Gloucestershire Regiment the poet Ivor Gurney was encamped near Oosthoek and wrote to his girlfriend, Marion Scott, from there in July 1917:

We have been transferred to a region where every plot of land is cultivated, where the country houses are grander than we are used to, where windmills invoke a sense of nostalgia and pride in the ingenuity of man. Churches and enormous houses stand out like beacons across a charming and delicate landscape. The atmosphere, Scarlatti or early Mozart like, is tranquil yet at the same time filled with heartache.

The windmill Gurney refers to was possibly *Steentje Mill* on the northern edge of the Galgebossen Wood, known to the military by a variety of names - Brake Wood, Tank Wood, Border Wood – but most commonly Slaughter Wood. The wood itself was the home of a number of camps. A nearby tavern gave its English translation as a name for Dirty Bucket Corner and Camp. A.30 Central, the British Army map reference for the camp between Poperinghe and Ypres was suited to the stationing of at least one divisional or brigade headquarters at any given time. Much later the camp boasted a Church Army Hut and a small cinema where the programme was often changed three times a week, with the officers paying four times the admission price of the ordinary ranks.

During the summer of 1917, in fields between Dirty Bucket Camp and Brandhoek beside the Elverdinghe road, a huge model of the front was constructed for company commanders and troops to familiarise themselves in preparation for their part in the coming Passchendaele offensive. Edmund Blunden described it as:

... an enormous model of the German systems now considered due to Britain was open for inspection, whether from the ground or from step ladders raised beside, and this was popular, though whether from its charm as a model or value as a military aid is uncertain.

Requested to visit this model, Edwin Campion Vaughan wrote:

After lunch Samuel came across and asked me if I would take a trip with him up towards the line. A large scale model of the front had been fashioned somewhere near Pop, and he wanted to find it so that he could take parties of officers to examine it. We went up on push-bikes, but foolishly did not ascertain where Divisional HQ was. We left our bikes in Pop at the APM's office and wandered about the open fields near Vlamertinghe until we arrived at Dirty Bucket Corner without having found the HQ or the model.

The following day, in company with fellow subalterns, Radcliffe and Harding, he found the model quite close to Slaughter Wood:

After about a mile we turned off towards Dirty Bucket Corner and shortly halted outside a wood wherein our camp lay. It was a nondescript camp consisting of bivouacs, tents, huts and tarpaulin shelters into which we stowed the troops as best we could. For our combined mess and bedroom we had a small hut with a table and a couple of forms. It was a baleful place for the shell-holes and shattered trees bore testimony to the attention of German gunners and the name of the camp was Slaughter Wood.

After an evening at La Poupée the three returned to camp a little the worse for drink; Vaughan was unable to sleep:

... so in pyjamas and slippers I went out again into the wood. A gentle rain was falling and the mud came up over my bare ankles. I had walked about thirty yards from the hut when without warning there was a blinding flash and a shell burst close beside me. Staggering back I hurried to the hut as three more crashed down among the trees. Kneeling on the steps I groped along the floor for my tin hat; at the same moment another salvo fell around us, chunks whizzed past my head and I heard the splintering of wood and a clatter as if the table had gone over.

Then I heard a voice screaming faintly from the bushes. Jamming on my tin hat I ran up the track and stumbled over a body. I stopped to raise the head but my hand sank into the open skull and I recoiled in horror. The cries continued and I ran on up the track to find that the water cart had been blown over on to two men. One was crushed and dead, the other pinned by the waist and legs. Other men ran up and we heaved the water cart up and had the injured man carried to the aid post. I took the papers and effects from the dead men and had the bodies moved into the bushes until morning then soaked with rain and covered with mud I returned to the hut.

August 14th - Each of us had had a miraculous escape. Over each bed was a hole through which had passed shrapnel and had any of the others been sitting up they would have been hit. A chunk had gone through my valise and would have gone through me had I been in bed. Three separate chunks must have missed my head by inches. The papers showed that one man was an HQ man, the other a sergeant from Trench Mortars.

Buried in nearby Hospital Farm Cemetery the two men were Private P. Rands, 1st/5th Battalion attached 143rd Trench Mortar Battery, Royal Warwickshire Regiment, and Sergeant. R. F. Worgan of the Gloucestershire Regiment. Buried beside them is Lance Corporal W. J. E. Burns, of the Machine Gun Corps who was killed at the same time.

Airfields were also prominent in the areas around Poperinghe. Constructed by the French in October 1914, Poperinghe Airfield was sited east of the town beside the road between Elverdinghe and Vlamertinghe. on large, open, pastureland. The ground was uneven, full of dips and hillocks, and the runway, such as it was, constantly deep in mud, and totally unsuitable for use in strong winds and heavy rain. On 22/23 April 1915 the airfield ceased operations after heavy shelling forced it to be abandoned. Shortly thereafter 't Hooghe Airfield was opened near the

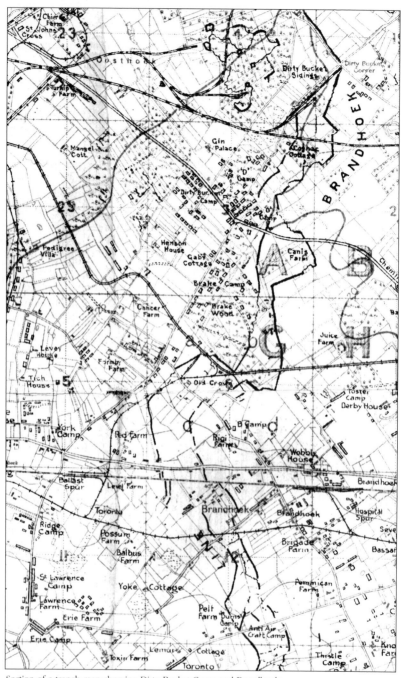

Section of a trench map showing Dirty Bucket Camp and Brandhoek

Poperinghe–Proven road. In early 1917, another, Droglandt Airfield, opened between Proven and the hamlet of Couthove, became the base for a Scout and two Artillery Squadrons, No.s. 7 and 9. In May, another, better known as La Lovie airfield, was opened beside the Proven-Krombeke road housing No.s. 19, Nieuport Scouts, and 71, Camel Scouts Squadrons.

The main purpose of La Lovie Airfield was to provide aerial protection for the La Lovie and Couthove Châteaux. At the former, General Ponsonby recorded:

February 28th 1916. Dined last night with Fatty Cavan (sic) at his Corps Hd. quarters, La Lovie Château at Proven. A magnificent Château with Ball Room etc. It is now occupied by a Belgian Count who bought it last year from the trustees of a Madame Vaughn, who inherited it from Leopold, Roi des Belges, with whom she lived in terms of great intimacy for many years. During dinner Madame la Comtesse played the piano next door. I was allowed to peep through the key-hole of the door and saw a very domestic scene. Monsieur le Comte, who ought to be fighting for his country, reading a book, la Comtesse playing high classical music, the two daughters and their governess working at the table, and a youth from school reading a novel.

During Third Ypres, La Lovie Château headquartered General Gough's Fifth Army. In July 1917, King George V stayed there during a visit to the region. Two months later, on 22 September, Gough, held to account for the lack of success and high losses during the Summer Offensive, was openly snubbed by Prime Minister David Lloyd George when, accompanied by General Charteris, he made an unannounced inspection visit.

Apart from the ever increasing bombardments of Poperinghe, 1917 was a year of tremendous activities in both the camps and the surrounding towns and villages. Movements of men and equipment were intensified while fuelling the Battle of Messines and Third Ypres, and, right up to November, the main road to Ypres was engulfed with an endless stream of motor lorries, caterpillar tractors hauling heavy guns, parties of troops on the march and countless GS Wagons heavily loaded with supplies – all moving forward for the final assaults on the Passchendaele Ridge. Vlamertinghe, by this time, was a partially-wrecked village, with almost every house more or less destroyed, and Poperinghe itself was suffering the results of countless shelling raids from long range guns.

Nevertheless, trade in the area flourished, with the shops, bars, estaminets and brothels continuing their roaring trade, enjoying a seemingly non-stop flow of customers.

Things were to change quite rapidly in the following year. 1918 was to see the death knell to this thriving 'economy'. The German offensive of that year was the beginning of the end of Poperinghe's role as the 'Capital of the Salient'. By May, every house and shop had been evacuated and the town was under constant bombardment. Shopkeepers were allowed into the town only to collect their stock-in- trade to enable them to re-establish themselves a mile or two back along the roads to the west. Here they built little shacks of wood, mud and any corrugated-iron or other materials they begged, borrowed or stole from the British Army. Some of them, like those of their counter-parts the refugees already there, were built entirely of tin boxes which once contained army biscuits.

Meanwhile a new line of trenches were under construction east of the town, part of a series of reserve trenches felt necessary to meet the anticipated advances of the enemy in the Ypres sector. At one time an enemy plane flew over this area and was met by a hail of bullets from Lewis guns, machine guns, rifles and revolvers which brought it down, albeit safely, near the Vlamertinghe Road. The pilot immediately jumped out and started to run towards his own lines, roughly four miles away. Not surprisingly, he was soon captured and brought back to his machine which was by then surrounded with British, French and Belgian soldiers, all claiming it as their prize. It all ended with a British Staff Captain placing a guard over it, declaring it a prize of the 148th Brigade, 49th West Riding Division.

Later in the year with the tables turned against the Imperial German Army, the conditions and activities in and around Poperinghe changed once again. During September and October the Poperinghe–Ypres road was flooded with refugees, leaving Poperinghe to return to their destroyed villages to reclaim their homes and farms and to start life anew. Roads into Poperinghe were likewise filled with its original population returning to pick-up their lives again.

In *Stand To, A Diary of the Trenches* Captain F. C. Hitchcock M.C., noted on returning to Poperinghe

... We overtook many families of refugees returning to "Pop", and to the numerous little wooden houses clotted along the edge of the road. Poperinghe, especially its square, presented a very battered appearance. The Hotel de Ville, and the house which "the Fancies" had used as a theatre, seemed to have suffered the most.

T. Lloyd wrote

Passing the railway station into the main thoroughfare, where many buildings appeared to be badly knocked about, the central part of "Pop" was astir as we entered. Something about the atmosphere that resembled a visit to a market town in England after a spell on a farm in the heart of the country. Prohibition, of necessity, must have existed during those past dark months, but today estaminets were open, supplying the needs of a thirsty, floating population, despite the 'heavies' falling at intervals on the outskirts... Barely a fortnight had elapsed since the state of acute danger had been removed, but during this brief interval the old town had undergone a decided transformation. For six months the population must have eked out a miserable existence away in some other neighbouring places removed from the danger-zone, where they patiently awaited the first favourable opportunity to return, and fervently hoped that their properties might be spared. Judging by the screened shops and estaminets that were being kept open until a late hour, most of these people had evidently returned and were now seemingly bent on making up for the lean past. Business was being carried out without restraint, and a fair number of troops and civilians paraded the streets.

Camps were emptying, Casualty Clearing Stations were being dismantled, labour gangs were moving-in to begin the work of returning the battlefields to a form suitable for civilians to inhabit. Supply dumps disappeared, only to reappear again as salvage dumps amply supplied from limbers moving down from Brandhoek Sidings where troops, struggling down from the front along miles of duckboard tracks had loaded them with machine guns, cartridge belts, shell-cases, steel helmets, rifles, bayonets, bombs and anything worth anything from the vast amount of battlefield rubbish left behind by both the retreating and advancing armies. Fields either side of the Poperinghe–Ypres road were gradually filled with rows of heavy artillery, machine-guns, howitzers, stacked rifles, vehicles, G.S. Waggons and all the now redundant equipment of war. The massive clearing-up operation and evacuation of armies and equipment was set in motion and the Imperial War Graves Commission teams had already long begun their grisly task of gathering and concentrating the dead.

After the Armistice, Poperinghe, with its damaged buildings soon rebuilt or repaired, returned to its more tranquil, civilian-dominated way of life, supplemented by a new influx of in-transit travellers.

In the post war years., thousands of ex-servicemen, and relatives and friends of those who fell on the battlefields of the Great War were to pass through Poperinghe to visit Talbot House or the military cemeteries. Again, local industry was to be partnered by a new one, the feeding, lodging and transporting of the bereft.

Today, things are pretty much the same in Poperinghe, although the visitors are mainly touring parties, descendants of those who fell, or students of the Great War, but the people of Poperinghe still welcome them in the same way.

Its the war that you'll find here
And the graves of thousands and thousands of soldiers
Always someone's father always someone's child...
W. Wermandere/G. Desimpelaere

9

GARDENS OF STONE

TODAY, POPERINGHE is a much larger town than it was during the war years. Agriculture and brewing activities have been supplemented by light industry, and there are few signs, although many buildings, thoroughfares and points of interest, recalling those war years. Traffic within the town can sometimes be compared with that during the war, but both of the old Switch Roads remain to ease traffic congestion within the town. As with most towns and villages on the old Western Front, the true and everlasting reminder of 1914–1918 is reflected in the military cemeteries in and around it.

All military cemeteries, wherever they may be, are places to reflect on the results of war, and they all have stories to tell of those individuals that lie buried within their walls. Those in Poperinghe and its surrounds tell, perhaps, sadder stories, in that the vast majority of those buried in them escaped the suddenness of death, and the sometimes misery and horror of dying on the battlefield, only to die while in the care of those dedicated to their well-being and aiding their recovery.

In the town itself there are three cemeteries, all in the avenue Deken de Bolaan: Poperinghe Communal Cemetery; Poperinghe Old Military Cemetery and Poperinghe New Military Cemetery.

Poperinghe Communal Cemetery was used by the British, French, and Belgian armies between October 1914 and March 1915.

Corporal Herbert Barrett, 'A' Company 2nd Battalion Worcestershire Regiment, killed on 21 October 1914 when only 26-years old, is believed to be the earliest known burial in the Ypres Salient.

The majority of the burials are those of officers brought into the Poperinghe Casualty Clearing Stations during First Ypres:

Imperial War Graves Commission gardener, Major Arthur J. Knowles, who died on 12 December 1921, aged 59, has a headstone featuring the cap-badge of the Queen's Westminster Rifles and the inscription:

Clean, Simple, Valiant, Well Beloved, Flawless In Faith And Fame.

The cemetery contains 23 British, 5 Imperial War Graves Commission, and 1 'Known Unto God' graves. The bodies of the French and Belgian soldiers that were originally buried in this cemetery were removed after the Armistice and the body of one British officer was removed to Ypres Reservoir Cemetery.

Poperinghe Old Military Cemetery is enclosed on all sides by a red brick wall, and beyond the right hand one can be seen the bedding of the old Hazebrouck–Poperinghe light railway. It was named Quintens Wandeling (Quinten's Walk), now a public footpath, after a local café-cum-bar by the railway sidings called *A la Promenade de Quintan*, Quintens Wandeling being the Flemish equivalent, From the sidings ran a light railway that serviced the camps and dumps along the southern side of the Poperinghe to Vlamertinghe road, before linking with the network of light railways that serviced the whole area behind the front line. The cemetery was begun in October 1914 to serve an emergency hospital in a château then located to the left of the cemetery. The château was damaged during the war, fell into disuse, and never rebuilt. Its cemetery was used by both British and French as an Aid Station, and from 1915 onwards, used for the burials of the civilian population, mostly typhoid victims; 500 were buried in the Château's kitchen garden. Most of the soldiers buried here fell during First Ypres, the Battle for Hill 60 in April/May 1915, and the gas attack on 22 April 1915. A few burials were made after the war.

The oldest burial is that of 29-year old Rifleman Harry Marriott, 2nd Battalion King's Royal Rifle Corps, who died on 23 October 1914. In a double grave, Marriott shares his last resting place with Guardsman A. Wardle of the Coldstream Guards, who died on 25 October 1914. The large

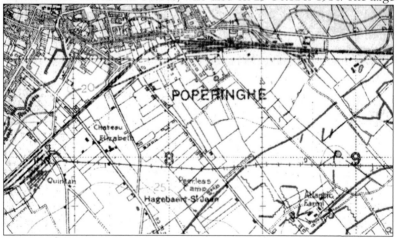

Quintan Sidings and the site of Château Elizabeth

central plot contains the burials from April–May 1915 of whom 30 are men of the King's Own Scottish Borderers, buried with their officer Captain Rupert C. Y. Dering, who died of wounds received in the fight for Hill 60 on 17–19 April 1915. Many of those who withstood the first German gas attack are also buried here, including Lieutenant-Colonel Boyle, Commanding 10th Battalion Canadian Infantry. By the end of May the cemetery was full and all further burials made in the New Military Cemetery.

In February 1919, Coolie 44735 Wang Ch'un Ch'ih murdered a colleague at the Chinese Labour Corps camp on the Scherpenberg. Executed on 8 May 1919 his headstone is inscribed:

A Good Reputation Endures Forever

800 French and Belgian soldiers and 500 Belgian civilians originally buried here were removed after the Armistice, hence the large space in front of the Great Cross.

The cemetery contains 397 British, 46 Canadian, 1 Chinese Labour Corps, 2 German, 22 British and 2 Canadian 'unknown' burials and special Memorials to 5 British and 2 Canadians "believed to be buried here".

Poperinghe New Military Cemetery, 200-yards further down the road, opposite the site of the old Château Elizabeth, was begun in June 1915 after the Old Military Cemetery was filled. It was used until the end of the war. Divided into French and British sections symbolising, it is said locally, the significant part played by both nations in the wartime defence of the town. In 1923, France awarded Poperinghe the Croix de Guerre. The French plot contains a number of headstones marking the graves of Islamic soldiers from France's African colonies. Among the crosses are two Belgian nurses, Martha Declercq and Euphrasie Vanneste, who both died in July 1917.

Telegraphist Harold Brooks, Royal Engineers (TA), tells the story of the death of his friend Henry William Hanna (First Class Honours, MSC. BSC. Manchester and Oxford Universities), and the grief of a brother, killed by a shell-burst and buried here:

29th February (1916). We have been plunged into gloom by the deaths of Harry Hawkins (sic) and 'Joe' Hanna, which occurred today. Whilst out with a working party. The day's work had been finished and the wagon had started on the return journey. A shell pitched about five yards from the back of the lorry and a splinter cut right through the floor, some slashed the side, and others went through the roof. Harry and Joe were on the tail board and caught the full force of the explosion. Joe pitched forward, killed instantly, but Harry lingered, apparently, for about an hour at the dressing station, happily, as far as anyone could judge, free from pain. Alf Coles and Trehearne both received slight wounds which were dressed on the spot.

How it was that nobody else was hurt is a miracle, as all the working party was packed into the lorry.

They were buried at the Military Cemetery on the Poperinghe - Reninghelst road, nearly opposite the Château Elizabeth. Life is cheap here, but as circumstances permit, the dead are given such honour as active service will allow. In the case of this funeral all men who were not actually on working parties or in action in the trenches were in attendance. Feeling was rather tense as we all gathered together before the parade. Everyone felt the blow very keenly, but none could comprehend the anguish of Alf Hawkins, (sic) it must have been a terrible ordeal for him. I with Bill Banton, Poole, and George Martin, acted as bearers to Joe. God grant that we do not have to go through such a ceremony again - it is terrible.

Sapper Henry George. Martin, one of his bearers was to be killed later in the war and now lies in the same cemetery.

Another instance, equally as poignant, occurred on 28 May 1916, when Canadian Army Service Corps Sergeant G. J. M. Pegg was mortally wounded on the verandah of Talbot House after writing a joint letter home with his brother. Another instance concerning brothers involved Private G. Ryan of the Hampshire Regiment, who died of wounds received at Potijze on 9 August 1916 - the register states "his brother, Private H. Ryan, was also

A soldier's burial at Poperinghe New Military Cemetery

killed on the same day." Lieutenant Edmund J. Maxwell-Stuart, 175th Tunnelling Company, Royal Engineers who was killed on 26 April 1916, was one of four brothers killed in the war

As well as eleven majors, there are a number of senior officers buried here, amongst them, four Lieutenant-Colonels: Raymond V. Doherty-Holwell, DSO., Royal Engineers and Assistant Director of Signals, VIII Corps Headquarters, he was killed 9 January 1917, Baronet Robert B.N. Gunter, 3rd Battalion Yorkshire Regiment, who died of wounds 16th August 1917, aged 46, and Herbert S. Smith, DSO, was killed 22 October 1915, whilst commanding the 1st Battalion the Leicestershire Regiment, G. H. Baker, 5th Canadian Mounted Rifles, aged 38; the son of a Canadian Senator and a member of the Canadian House of Commons, was mortally wounded during the German attacks on Hill 62, on 2 June 1916.

Captain Hugh H. Maclean of the Highland Light Infantry, acting as Brigade-Major, he was killed by shellfire which mortally wounded his GOC Brigadier General A. F. Gordon, Captain James H. W. Hay was killed while acting as Adjutant to 9th Battalion, Seaforth Highlanders, on 30 November 1917.

This cemetery has gained notoriety in containing the highest number of executed men anywhere on the western front. Plot II houses 17 such graves. Two Canadians: the first, Irish immigrant Private James H. Wilson, 4th Battalion Canadian Infantry, deserted on 13 June 1916, during the fighting around Mount Sorrel., and was executed on 9 July, and the second Private Comte LaLiberte, 3rd Battalion Canadian Infantry, also deserted during the Mount Sorrel fighting and was executed on 4 August. Private John Bennett, 1st. Battalion Hampshire Regiment having experienced the slaughter of the July battles on the Somme – the battalion lost 585 men on the first day – lost his nerve and deserted on 8 August during a German gas attack in the salient (this alone resulted in the 101 men of the 4th and 29th Divisions being buried at Lijssenthoek Cemetery). Subsequently charged with cowardice in the face of the enemy, he was executed on 28 August.

Private Albert Botfield, 9th Battalion South Staffordshire Regiment had deserted from an entrenching party near Contalmaison, Somme, on 21 September. After his Division had moved north he was tried for cowardice, found guilty, and executed on 18 October in the inner courtyard of Poperinghe Town Hall. Private Richard Stevenson, 1/4th Loyal North Lancashire Regiment, deserted 7 September from the fighting around Fricourt. He was captured four days later and was executed on 25 October. Private Bernard McGeehan, 1st/8th King's Regiment, was under arrest for desertion when his division moved up to the salient and was executed on 2 November. Private Reginald Tite, 13th Royal Sussex Regiment was

Plot II at Poperinghe New Military Cemetery houses 17 graves of those who were executed

charged with cowardice after deserting from the trenches near Thiepval. Tried on the Somme on 2 November, he was executed at Wormhoudt, Northern France, and brought for burial to Poperinghe in the back of a lorry. Private William H. Simmonds, 23rd Battalion Middlesex Regiment, another Somme deserter, also had to wait until his division moved north before being tried. He was executed on 1 December. 31 year old Second-Lieutenant Eric S. Poole, 11th West Yorkshire Regiment, was one of only three officers to be executed during the war. Returning to duty, after previously being wounded by shrapnel, Second-Lieutenant Poole constantly suffered bouts of hesitancy and disorientation. However, after deserting from his battalion's trenches near Bailleul, his plea of shell-shock at his trial on November 21 went unheeded. Charged with cowardice in the face of the enemy, he was found guilty and was executed at Poperinghe town hall on 10 December 1916.

The first execution of 1917, Private James Crampton, 9th Battalion Yorks & Lancaster Regiment, took place on 4 February. Attached to a Royal Engineers unit, Crampton deserted from the front line in the vicinity of Armentières. Private John W. Fryer, 12th Battalion East Surrey Regiment, already under a suspended death sentence for desertion, deserted again when the battalion moved into the trenches around St. Eloi. He was executed on 14 June. Private James S. Michael, 10th Cameronians (Scottish Rifles), deserted and evaded capture for a few months before being picked up. Returned to his Division, the 15th Scottish, in time for its part in the attack on Pilckem Ridge on 31 July 1917, he was executed three weeks later on 24 August. Complaining that he could no longer stand the constant bombardments Private Joseph Stedman, 117th Machine Gun Company, walked away from a newly captured German trench near St. Julian on 1 August, and was executed five weeks later on 5 September. Sergeant John T. Wall, 3rd Battalion Worcestershire Regiment, had seen continuous action since 1914, serving with the battalion when it suffered huge losses on the Bellewaerde Ridge in 1915. On 17 August – two years later – the Worcesters were back on the ridge and Sergeant Wall deserted. He was executed on 6 September. A persistent absconder, Private George Everill, 1st Battalion North Staffordshire Regiment, finally ran out of luck after deserting from Dickebusch on 24 August, when his regiment was warned for the trenches. Captured the following day, he was shot on the 14 September. 17-year old Jamaican, Private Herbert Morris, British West Indies Regiment was terrified of shellfire. Receiving no assistance from the battalion medical officer, when his company was deployed in the vicinity of Burnt Farm, he deserted. Herbert Morris, despite not being old enough to serve overseas, was executed in Poperinghe. The last executee to be buried here was a regular soldier, Private Frederick C. Gore, 7th Battalion East Kent Regiment. He had been charged with cowardice, and deserted twice previously. Pleading that his nerves cracked every time he faced heavy bombardments, gained no favour from the medical officer or the court martial officers. He was shot at dawn on 16 October 1917.

Staff Sergeant James Pick, Royal Army Service Corps was murdered on 11 February 1916;. His killer, Driver Thomas Moore, was executed at nearby Busseboom on 26 February. After the war, Moore's body could not be found and he is commemorated on the Menin Gate in Ypres.

The cemetery contains 596 British, 275 French, 55 Canadian, 20 Australian, 3 New Zealand, 2 British West Indies, 1 Chinese Labour Corps, and 1 German, burials. After the Armistice 118 Belgian burials were removed.

Nine Elms British Cemetery, just west of Poperinghe, was begun on 16 September 1917 to serve the many Casualty Clearing Stations thereabouts, particularly the 3rd Australian and No. 44 Casualty Clearing Stations which operated here after their removal from Brandhoek in late August 1917. The name Nine Elms, deriving from an avenue in Lambeth, originates from a London unit camped nearby in 1915. One section of plots contain burials from the 1918 German Spring Offensive and the September breakout from the Salient. A separate plot contains burials of, mostly, German prisoners of war who died between September 1917 and March 1918. 95 American and a number of French graves were removed after the Armistice. The space created by the latter removal, was used in May 1940 for the burial of 22 British soldiers. The 95 Americans, men of the 30th (Tennessee) Division, based at Vogelte Farm close by the cemetery, died in the action at Vierstraat on 1st September, when they and their sister American 27th (New York) Division, were attached to the British Second Army.

Two executed soldiers are buried here. Private J. Nisbet, 1st Battalion Leicestershire Regiment, already under a suspended death sentence for attempted desertion, absconded a second time whilst his unit were moving up to the front He was executed on 23 August 1918. Private J. MacFarlane, 4th King's Regiment was executed for desertion on 22 May 1918.

Private J. H. Edgerton, Australian Machine Gun Corps (with service number 44), died of wounds 5 October 1917, his headstone is inscribed

He Died As He Lived, A Soldier And A Man.
Father And Mother.

The following relates to the death of Rifleman W. D. Sutherland, A.I.F.:

Dear Sir (Sutherland's father),

I am writing to tell you about your son, Rifleman W.D. Sutherland, 39912.

He was brought into this hospital on the 8th, very collapsed, suffering from a severe shell wound in his right arm and chest which penetrated his lungs, also one of his legs. He was immediately warmed up and made comfortable in bed, but the injury done to his lung had been too severe; he never really picked up at all, and died on the morning of the 11th. I am afraid it is not very much to tell you, but it might be some comfort to his people to know that he was in hospital where he received every possible care and attention, and that he was relieved of all his pain. I told him when he was first brought in not to worry, that I would write and tell you that he was wounded, and he was very relieved. He sent his love to everyone and hoped soon to be well enough to write himself. He had no idea at all that he was dying. He was buried today in a military cemetery at 'Nine Elms', near Poperinghe. All his personal belongings will eventually be sent to you. I remain,
Yours Faithfully,
Ida O'Dayer
(Sister in Charge).

The cemetery contains 955 British, 149 Australian, 1 Bermudan, 2 British West Indies, 289 Canadian, 8 Guernsey, 1 Indian, 7 New Foundland, 118 New Zealand, 26 South African, 37 German and 22 World War II, burials.

Gwalia Cemetery, a short distance from Poperinghe on the road to Elverdinghe, took its name from Gwalia Farm Hospital and served as the burial ground for the Main Dressing Station sited there in June 1917. It remained in use until September 1918, the end of the fighting in the Salient. It is highly likely that the farm received its name from a battalion encamped here prior to 1917 whose regimental honours include the 1858 Battle of Gwalior which concluded the Indian Mutiny. As elsewhere behind the lines, the majority of burials here are artillerymen, many of them Royal Marines. There are also 30 Royal Engineers and 30 men of the Royal Army Service Corps.

Buried here is Lieutenant-Colonel Percy W. Beresford, D.S.O., twice Mentioned in Despatches, who died of wounds received whilst commanding the 2/3rd Battalion London Regiment, on 26 October 1917, aged 42, and Chaplain 4th Class, the Reverend Cecil Langdon attached 11th Border Regiment, who was killed in action 31 October 1917, aged 35. Killed in action on 26th May 1918, Second-Lieutenant William D. R. Parsons, 16th Battalion (The Queen's) Royal West Surrey Regiment, lies beside 8 Privates of his regiment who were killed on the same day.

The numerous camps and artillery batteries surrounding Gwalia Farm Hospital, and with Dirty Bucket Camp situated a few hundred yards eastwards, caused the area to be a favourite target for enemy shelling. On 4 July 1917, 'C' Battalion, Tank Corps were in rest there when heavy

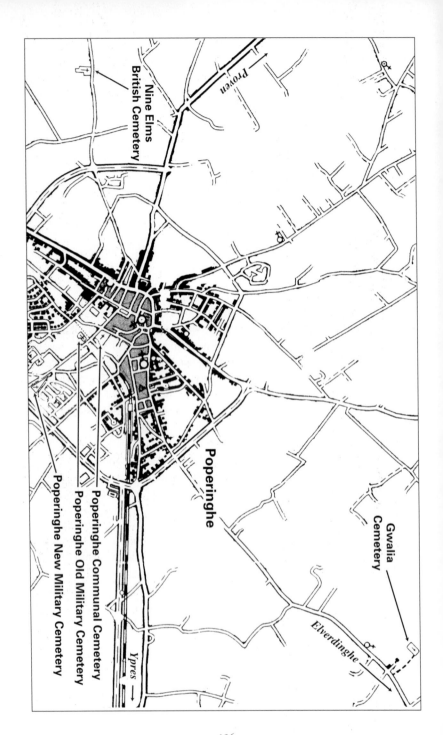

Nine Elms
British Cemetery

Proven

Poperinghe

Gwalia
Cemetery

Poperinghe Communal Cemetery
Poperinghe Old Military Cemetery
Poperinghe New Military Cemetery

Ypres

Elverdinghe

126

shelling destroyed the battalion orderly room, killing five men and wounding four. Three months later, 34th brigade were in rest here when, during the night of 4 October, an air raid claimed the lives of 14 men of the 9th Battalion Lancashire Fusiliers who today lie buried in Plot I.

Colonel David Rorie, while stationed at Gwalia Farm Hospital in 1917, gives an account which highlights the efficiency of the Imperial War Graves Commission personnel at the time, as well as giving some indication of what he thought of some members of the Chaplain's Department:

Padrés abounded at the Corps M.D.S.: barring the Salvation Army I think we had all the known varieties, and several of each at that – Presbyterian (Scots and English), R.C., Wesleyan and C. of E. As they swamped us out of our mess table, we, the sons of Galan, holding only to our proven and divisional spiritual advisers, had to give the rest a long table to themselves. This was popularly known as "The General Assembly," and they sat and discussed the mess cook and moot points of theology. One was under a cloud: he had buried a Malay in the Chinese cemetery, and later had to disinter him and put him in his proper place at the irate demand of a Graves Commission warrior of Irish extraction: even to death there is no satisfactory blending of Mahomet with Confucius.

The cemetery contains 444 British, 14 British West Indies, 5 New Zealand, 4 Chinese Labour Corps, 2 Australian, 1 South African, and 3 German burials.

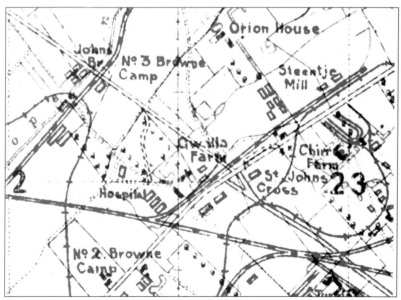

Gwalia Farm and its surrounding camps and Casualty Clearing Stations

Brandhoek, on the Poperinghe–Ypres road, houses three British Military Cemeteries: Brandhoek Military Cemetery; Brandhoek New Military Cemetery and Brandhoek New Military Cemetery No 3.

Brandhoek Military Cemetery opened next to an Advanced Dressing Station during Second Ypres. Its first burials, mostly gas victims, were made in May 1915. By July 1917 the site was full, the cemetery closed and the Advanced Dressing Station was replaced by three Casualty Clearing Stations,

The high proportion of Artillery burials here is evidence of the many gun batteries situated around the village, Second-Lieutenant John S. Leeds, 1st Honourable Artillery Company, who died on 19 September 1915, aged 28, enlisted in September 1914, having returned from Argentina to do so. His colleague in the 1st H.A. C., former Daily Chronicle reporter Private George Mascord, aged 26, died of wounds the following day. Five days later, on 25 September, Second-Lieutenant Rowland T. Cobbold aged 23, another who returned from Argentina to enlist, was killed in action whilst serving with the 6th Battery Royal Field Artillery.

Killed when their observation balloon was destroyed on 16 July 1917, Royal Flying Corps officers Captain Edward A. Wickson and Lieutenant Thomas F. Lucas lie next to each other. The cemetery also contains some of the higher-ranked older men who served: Brigadier-General F. J. Heyworth, C.B., D.S.O., of the Scots Guards was killed in action on 9 May 1916 whilst commanding the 3rd Guards Brigade; Lieutenant-Colonel Arthur F. Sargeaunt, Royal Engineers was killed 31 July 1917, aged 44, and Lieutenant-Colonel James Clarke, C.B., 1st/9th Battalion, Argyll and Sutherland Highlanders, died of wounds on 10 May 1915, aged 56. Boer War veteran, Colonel Charles Conyers, aged 46 who, while serving with the 2nd Battalion Royal Irish Fusiliers, was killed when leading a charge of the 2nd Leinsters at St. Eloi on 12 May 1915.

The cemetery contains 601 British, 63 Canadian, 4 Australian, 2 Bermudan and 2 German burials.

Brandhoek New Military Cemetery was started in July 1917 following the closure of the Brandhoek Military Cemetery; serving the 3rd (Australian), No. 32 and No. 44 Casualty Clearing Stations until their closure in August, by which time the site had become full, and another cemetery was opened nearby. This cemetery is the only Commonwealth War Graves Commission cemetery containing a headstone inscribed with two Victoria Crosses. Captain Noel Godfrey Chavasse, Royal Army Medical Corps, attached King's (Liverpool Scottish) Regiment, won both of his during the Great War. He was awarded the Military Cross for acts of bravery during the fighting around Hooge in 1915. A year later, on 9 August 1916, he was awarded the

Victoria Cross at Guillemont on the Somme. He was awarded the Bar posthumously after his death on 4 August 1917 during First Ypres. On the first day of the battle he was seen standing and waving to soldiers, indicating his Aid Post at Bossaert Farm, about 500 yards past Wieltje. He was hit in the head by a shell splinter, but was able to walk to Wieltje Farm Dressing Station to get the wound dressed. Refusing further treatment he returned to his post.

Early on 1 August, a queue of the wounded were outside of his Aid Post, while he was seen to be working with a captured German medical officer to whom he constantly remarked 'Good fellow, fine fellow.' At some point during the day he was hit twice in the head, and was found sitting in six-inches of water with a bandage round his head. Shortly after, he was wounded again. At 1 o'clock on the afternoon of 4 August 1917, he died. The sister who nursed him through his last hours wrote:

> He was buried next day, a large number of Officers, Sisters, medical men present, near here. He lies in a large field with a little cross with his name upon it and in time it will be very nicely laid out, when the Huns have given up shelling over the field. No special arrangements were made for his burial, but the whole Battalion paraded, as did all the Medical Officers of the hospital.

His headstone bears the inscription:

Greater Love Hath No Man Than This,
That A Man Lay Down His Life For His Friends.

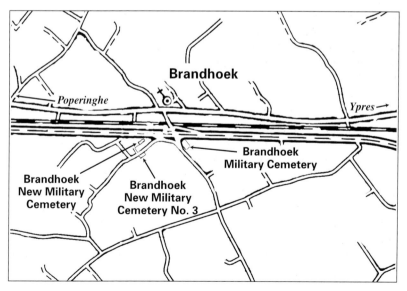

Only three men have ever won the Victoria Cross twice – Captain Chavasse, Lieutenant-Colonel A. Martin-Leake RAMC who was awarded one in the Boer War, and the Bar at White Château during First Ypres, and Captain C. H. Upham who won both in the Second World War.

Buried next to Chavasse is 19 year-old Second-Lieutenant Frederick J.

Wright, 1st/8th King's Liverpool Regiment, who died the same day, and Chavasse's servant, Private C. A. Rudd, killed on 10 August, aged 20, is buried a few feet away. Two other medical officers buried here are, Captain Frank R. Armitage, D.S.O., attached 232rd Brigade Royal Field Artillery, who died of wounds on 30 July 1917, and Captain Hugh D. Willis attached 3rd Battalion Worcestershire Regiment, died of wounds on 12 August 1917. There is a predominance of Irish regiments here including a battalion commander, Lieutenant-Colonel T. H. Boardman, D.S.O., 8th Battalion Inniskilling Fusiliers, who died of wounds on 5 August 1917, and 38 year-old Mons veteran, Company Sergeant-Major E. Power, M.C., who died of wounds 8 August. A regular of 2nd Battalion Royal Irish Regiment, he was the holder of the

The headstone of Captain Noel G. Chavasse

Military Cross, an award rarely granted to warrant officers.

There are a high proportion of artillery burials within the cemetery which contains 514 British, 11 Australian, 6 Canadian, and 28 German burials.

Brandhoek New Military Cemetery No. 3 began when Brandhoek New Military Cemetery became full. It remained in use until May 1918. The bronze cemetery gates were the gift of Mr. G. H. Strutt, father of Lieutenant Anthony H. Strutt, 16th Battalion (Chatsworth Rifles) Sherwood Foresters, who died in one of the Casualty Clearing Stations here on 27 April 1918. There are two senior officers:. Lieutenant-Colonel T. C. Irving, D.S.O., Staff Officer with 4th (Canadian) Division Engineers, who died of wounds on 29 October 1917, aged 38, and 46 year-old Lieutenant-Colonel Stafford

James Somerville; a long-serving officer of 1st Inniskilling Fusiliers. He was attached to 9th Battalion Royal Irish Fusiliers when he died of wounds received near the Steenbeek on 16 August 1917.

Buried alongside each other are brothers Corporal. W. Bathgate of the 113th Field Ambulance, who died of wounds on 15 August 1917, and Sergeant Robert Bathgate of the 112th Field Ambulance who died 31 October.

Of the 966 burials here 286 are artillerymen. The cemetery contains 849 British, 46 Australian, 46 Canadian, 18 New Zealand, 5 South African, 1 British West Indies, and 1 Chinese Labour Corps burials. 4 French burials were removed after the armistice.

Mendinghem British Cemetery, at Proven, approximately 4 miles north of Poperinghe is one of three Casualty Clearing Station complexes with a name determined by the soldier's humour rather than by association with its siting or regiment. Although the cemetery was begun in June 1916 when No. 46 Casualty Clearing Station was sited here, the first burials were not made until August after which it was in regular use until September 1918. The Station was set up specifically to deal with gas cases and head wounds,

A recipient of the Victoria Cross is buried here, acting Lieutenant-Colonel Captain Bertram Best-Dunkley, who died of wounds on 5 August 1917. His citation reads:

The London Gazette, 6 September 1917.

... late Lancashire Fusiliers... when in command of his battalion, the leading waves of which, during an attack, became disorganised by reason of rifle

Mendinghem British Cemetery, Proven

Mendinghem British Cemetery, Proven

and machine-gun fire at close range from positions which were believed to be in our hands. Lieutenant-Colonel Best-Dunkley dashed forward, rallied his leading waves, and personally led them to the assault of these positions, which, despite heavy losses, were carried. He continued to lead his battalion until all their objectives had been gained. Had it not been for this officer's gallant and determined action it is doubtful if the left of the brigade would have reached its objectives. Later in the day, when our position was threatened he collected his battalion headquarters, led them to the attack, and beat off the advancing enemy. This gallant officer has since died of wounds.

There are three men buried here who were executed for desertion: Private John J. Hyde, 10th King's Royal Rifle Corps on 5 September 1917; Private Charles Britton, 1/5th Royal Warwicks, deserting at the end of July 1917, he was arrested just over two weeks later on August 16 and executed on 12 September, and Private David Gibson, 12th Royal Scots who, on failing to return from leave, was arrested in the UK, returned to Flanders, and was tried and executed on 24 September 1918, aged 25.

The cemetery contains 2,272 British, 33 South African, 28 Canadian, 26 British West Indies, 15 Australian, 12 New Zealand, 3 New Foundland, 8 Chinese Labour Corps, and 51 German burials.

Haringhe (Bandagehem) British Cemetery, in the village of **Haringhe**, approximately 8-miles northwest of Poperinghe, another Casualty Clearing Station complex given its nickname by troops to suit their humour. Casualty Clearing Stations were set up here during the 1917 Summer Offensive.

Three winners of the Albert Medal are in this cemetery: 31-year old Company Sergeant Major Albert H. Furlonger, D.C.M.; 25-year old Sapper George E. Johnson and Sapper Joseph C. Farren, Royal Engineers of the 29th, 21st and 12th Light Railway Operating Companies respectively. Their medals were awarded for acts of heroism on 30 April 1918, when they were manning an ammunition train as it arrived at a refuelling depot. They had just uncoupled the engine, when the second truck burst into flames. Furlonger immediately ordered the driver, Bigland (also awarded the Albert Medal), to move the engine back and pull-away the two trucks nearest to it. Without hesitation Bigland did so. Furlonger coupled the engine himself and Woodman (a fifth winner of the Albert Medal in this incident), uncoupled the burning truck. The two trucks were drawn clear of the ammunition dump, but the ammunition exploded, wrecking the engine and both trucks, killing Furlonger, Farren, and Johnson, and seriously wounding Bigland. The London Gazette citation reads:

Had it not been for the courageous action of these men, whereby three of them lost their lives and one was seriously injured, there is not the slightest

Haringhe (Bandagehem) British Cemetery, Haringe

134

doubt that the whole dump would have been destroyed and many lives lost.

At the rear of the cemetery, the grave of French civilian Louis Senjean is next to Quartermaster Sergeant. W. D. Ward, Australian Engineers, who both died on 17 April 1918.

After the Armistice 4 British, 4 French, and 1 German, plus 2 American and 2 Belgian graves, were removed. 5 British burials were added during the Second World War.

Dozinghem Military Cemetery was set up in the village of Westvleteren to serve the Casualty Clearing Stations sited there from July 1917 onwards. This is the third cemetery complex named to fit the humour of the British soldier. This part of Belgium was never in the British sector, and the cemetery is its only link with British forces, other than a narrow gauge railway that ran from it to Poperinghe five-miles away. Most of those who lie here had arrived with inoperable wounds. Dr. Harvey Cushing, stationed nearby at Mendinghem, was a regular visitor to Dozinghem, having many friends and colleagues on the staff. On Thursday 30 August 1917, his visit was made to find Edward Revere Osler, the son of an eminent London Surgeon and descendent of Paul Revere, the man who, in 1775, made the famous ride from Boston to Lexington Green to warn the rebelling 'colonials' that "The redcoats are coming":

Last Sunday (26th) came a letter from Lady Osler telling me that Revere was somewhere near St. Julien and how dreadful it would be should he be brought in to me with a head wound, and yet how thankful they would be. I answered immediately, asking her to wire me the number of his unit so that I could try and locate him among the millions. Rather used up, I was preparing to turn in at 10 last night, when came this shocking message: 'Sir Wm. Osler's son seriously wounded at 47 CCS Can Major Cushing come immediately?' The CO let me have an ambulance, and we reached Dosinghem in about half an hour. It could not have been much worse, though there was a bare chance – one traversing through the upper abdomen, another penetrating the chest just above the heart, two others in the thigh, fortunately without a fracture.

The local CO would not let me cable, and I finally insisted on phoning GHQ – got General Macpherson on the wire and persuaded him to send to Oxford via the London War Office: 'Revere seriously wounded: not hopelessly: conscious: comfortable.'

Crile came over from Remy with Eisenberry, and after transfusion, Darrach, assisted by Brewer, opened the abdomen about midnight. There had been bleeding from two holes - in the upper colon and the mesenteric vessels. His condition remained unaltered, and about seven this morning the world lost this fine boy, as it does many others every day.

We saw him buried in the early morning. A soggy Flanders field beside a little oak grove to the rear of the Dosinghem group – an overcast, windy, autumnal day – the long rows of simple wooden crosses – the new ditches half full of water being dug by Chinese coolies wearing tin helmets – the boy wrapped in an army blanket and covered by a weather-worn Union Jack, carried on their shoulders by four slipping stretcher bearers. A strange scene – the great, great grandson of Paul Revere under a British flag, and awaiting him a group of some six or eight American Army medical officers – saddened with the thoughts of his father. Happily it was a dry day at this end of the trench, and some green branches were thrown in for him to lie on. The Padré recited the usual service – the bugler gave the 'Last Post' – and we went about our duties, Plot 4, Row F.

Major Batchelor, the CO of A Battery, 59th Brigade, and seven men had been brought in at the same time, as I learned from the records. I saw and talked with several of them during the evening. They were just beyond Pilckem, between Langemarck and St. Julien, two or three hundred yards this side of Hindenburg Trench, and were preparing to move the four batteries up today. Major Batchelor, Revere, and eighteen men were bridging over a shell hole in preparation for the move of the guns in their battery. It was about 4.30 in the afternoon and there had been no shelling. They were so busy they did not even hear the first shell – a direct hit which wounded eight out of the twenty.

It was difficult to get back, but they finally were brought to the Dressing Station at Essex Farm on the canal – a 3000-yard carry, then a short distance on a narrow-gauge ammunition track – the advanced post of the 131st Field Ambulance in front of Canada Farm, then by ambulance to No. 47, which was 'taking in' - a matter of four hours.

Dozinghem Military Cemetery, Westvleteren

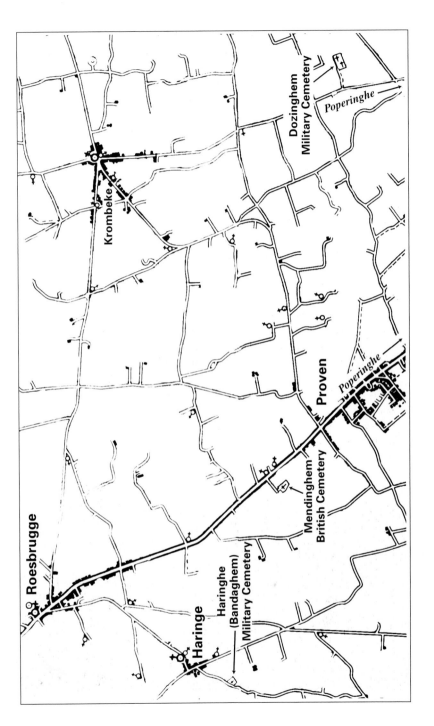

The brothers Trapp: Stanley, 8 Squadron RNAS; George, 10 Squadron RNAS, and Donovan, 85 Squadron RAF died in December 1916, November 1917 and September 1918 respectively. Ray Collishaw, Commanding 10 Squadron in 1917, who was to become a top ace in the war, wrote *Air Command,* a book on George Trapp, and married one of his sisters.

The cemetery holds 3,021 British, 61 Canadian, 34 British West Indies, 19 New Foundland, 15 South African, 14 New Zealand, 6 Australian, 3 Chinese, 1 Known Unto God, 65 German, and 73 Second World War burials

Grootebeek British Cemetery, originally named Ouderdom British Cemetery after the village it rests in, is considered to be one of the most beautiful cemeteries in the salient, sited on an island surrounded by the Grootebeek stream from which it takes its name.

On 23/24 April 1915, the 13th Infantry Brigade, 1st Canadian Division, and Lahore Division were rushed from their rest camps near Ouderdom to breach the gap in the line between Wieltje and St Julien where the Germans had first used chlorine gas on the 22nd. The Lahore Division distinguished itself on the 26 when:

Grootebeek British Cemetery

... .at 2 o'clock, two brigades advanced upon the enemy at Mauser Ridge and came under appalling fire. Their ranks were depleted, but they pushed forward, leaving their dead in great heaps. Just as they came to the wire a cloud of gas was released, blowing across the advancing troops. The 40th Pathans and 47th Sikhs held on, though some of the Indians, all having no protection from gas, fell back. The Lahore Division consolidated the line'.

There are 7 men of the Lahore Division buried here.

To the left of the Great Cross is a special memorial headstone in memory of Private J. Lynn D.C.M., V.C., 2nd Lancashire Fusiliers. Killed on 2 May 1915, he was buried in Vlamertinghe Churchyard but his grave was lost in later battles. His story is told in *Deeds That Thrill The Empire*.

The cemetery contains 97 British, 7 Indian, 1 Bermuda, 1 New Zealand, 1 South African, I Unnamed, and 21 Second World War burials.

Reninghelst New Military Cemetery, approximately 4-miles south of Poperinghe, was begun in November 1917 in a field next to the local Boy's School which, at the time, was housing a Field Ambulance. One third of the burials here are of artillerymen.

Brigadier-General Charles W. E. Gordon, 17th Battalion Black Watch, Commanding 123rd (London) Brigade, was buried here having been killed on 23 July whilst inspecting the line near Spoil Bank.

Billeted in the village during the spring of 1916, the Canadian 3rd Division suffered highly in the June fighting around Mount Sorrel, and a large number of them are buried here, including brothers Lieutenants Charles R. and John L. Godwin.

Three of the executed are buried here. Private R. L. Barker, 6th Battalion London Regiment, executed for cowardice on 4 November 1916, Private F. Loader, 1st/22nd London Regiment, executed on 19 August 1917 for desertion, and Private W. Smith, 3rd/5th Lancashire Fusiliers, who deserted with two others from the trenches between Frezenberg Ridge and Poelcappelle on 4 October 1917. Surrendering three days later Smith was executed on 14 November. the only one of the three to be so.

The cemetery contains 452 British, 230 Canadian, 104 Australian, 7 Chinese Labour Corps, 2 New Zealand, 1 South African, 2 German, 1 British Civilian, and 1 Known Unto God, burials.

Reninghelst Churchyard and Extension Cemetery in the centre of the village was begun with three burials in the churchyard during the early stages of Second Ypres. The adjoining Extension, although only used for a short time, was rapidly filled during May 1915.

On 1 May, the Germans launched a gas attack at Hill 60, then defended by troops of the British 5th Division. Many of the wounded were taken to No.15 Field Ambulance sited in a school behind the church. On 2 and 3

May, 12 1st Dorsets and one 1st Bedfords died here. A gas and infantry attack on 5 May secured the hill for the enemy; a position they held until June 1917. The casualties suffered by the 5th Division are evident throughout the cemeteries hereabouts. Between 5 and 7 May, a further 11 of their number from the 2nd Duke of Wellington's Regiment died. By the late autumn of 1915 a further 30 burials had almost filled the cemetery.

The last burial here was Reverend M. Bergin, M.C., an Irish Jesuit chaplain serving with the Australian Army, killed on 12 October 1917 near Zonnebeke. Padré Achiel van Walleghem officiated at the funeral:

> The funeral of Father Bergin is at 11 o'clock, after the English mass. With 8 priests in attendance (3 army padrés and 5 priests presently resident in Reninghelst) it was done as solemnly as possible. Affording full military honours to the proceedings a number of soldiers accompanied the coffin. His body rests just outside the churchyard hedge, opposite the brewery.

The cemetery contains 55 British, 1 Australian, 2 Second World War burials, and 1 special memorial to a British soldier whose grave was lost.

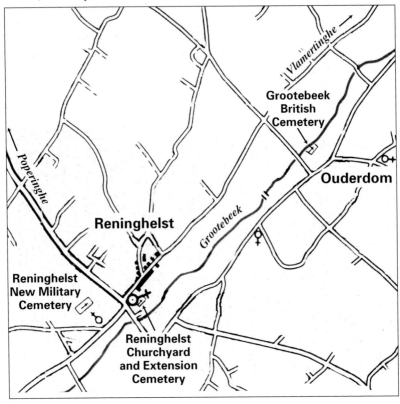

Lijssenthoek Military Cemetery, southwest of Poperinghe on the road that was once the Poperinghe–Hazebrouck railway line, with 10,802 burials is the second largest cemetery in the Salient. Only Tyne Cot Cemetery, Passchendaele with 11,908 burials is larger. Lijssenthoek, or Remy Sidings as it was called during the war, was the largest British burial ground on the Western Front. As one of the cemeteries in the Commonwealth War Graves Commission's 'First Priority Programme' it was made ready in time for King George V's visit to the Western Front in May 1922 . Its designer, Sir Reginald Blomfield, then overseeing the construction of 40 cemeteries in the Salient, was frustrated by the lack of time, money and space he could command in order to give his cemeteries a sense of grandeur. At Lijssenthoek, he was able to achieve what is widely considered to be his masterpiece. He combined nature with grandeur by simply changing the position of the entrance. During the war, the dead were brought into the cemetery by an entrance near Remy Farm, known as the French Gate. Blomfield positioned his entrance on long, wisteria-covered terraces directing attention to the War Stone. A shelter, in the style of the entrance 100 yards further on, helps give the impression of entering a huge garden of stone, shrubs and flowers.

Prior to the construction of the cemeteries, many of the burial grounds

Remy Sidings alongside Remy Farm, with the old Poperinghe–Hazebrouck railway line replaced by a road, still shows signs of the original embankment upon which the road was built

had been tended by soldiers, caring for their comrades graves, and often visiting them before returning to the front line. The transformation of the many burial grounds into reminders of English country gardens was born of their example. After the war, many of these soldiers joined the ranks of the newly formed Imperial War Graves Commission. One of the first gardeners at Lijssenthoek, Thomas McGrath, formerly of the 2nd Battalion Lancashire Regiment, married a local girl, Maria of Café Remy, Poperinghe. Buried to the left of the main entrance he died of sickness on 23 April 1920. Another, Walter Sutherland, who planted the two Canadian cedar trees shading the War Stone, married his Belgian sweetheart, Marie Lermyte, whose family owned the Café Boonaert opposite the Great Cross. The couple settled down in the town and raised a family. Their son George and grandson Alex, followed in Walter's footsteps as gardeners at Lijssenthoek. George, speaking of his father said:

> He wanted to forget but he couldn't. Those who were still alive after the war, such as my father, thought that they had a duty to perform and to take care of the graves.

The oldest burials date from May-June 1915 when the French 15th Evacuation Hospital was sited here. Plots I to XII contain all the 1915 to 1916 British burials with the officers, at that time buried separately, in rows IA, IIA, VA, VIA, XA and IXB. This distinction, repeated again in 1917, was

A Canadian cedar tree planted by gardener Walter Sutherland shading the War Stone at Lijssenthoek

not the norm, making the burials at Lijssenthoek almost unique. During the 1917 summer offensive, the number of burials increased dramatically with the result that the plots spread further along the Boeschepe road and back towards the Winterbeek stream bordering the farm. In the spring of 1918 a large number of French burials were made to the left of the present entrance and at the back near the farm. To the right of the entrance, and at the rear of the cemetery, 76 headstones record the burials of 223 German prisoners of war, many of them in mass graves, who either died of wounds, or whilst engaged in clearing the battlefields after the war. The latter fate also befell most of the 35 Chinese Labour Corps members buried in Plot XXXIV. Of the 50 American servicemen buried here by 1918, 47 were either repatriated or reburied in the In Flanders Fields Cemetery at Waregem in the 1920s. The remaining three found in the small semi-circle of graves left of the main entrance, are the only American burials in the Salient. New York Private Harry King, was killed by one of the last long range shells fired in the salient whilst on traffic control duty at Watou on 20 September 1918.

Private Donald Snaddon, 1st Battalion Royal Scots, was only 15 when he died on 18 January 1916. Buried next to him is Pioneer William Waple of the Royal Engineers, who, at 52, was over the eligible age for military service when he died of appendicitus on the same day.

Private William Baker, 26th Battalion Royal Fusiliers was sentenced to

Remy Farm, with the French burials, at the back of the cemetery

death after several attempts at desertion during the German Spring Offensive of 1918. Executed in Poperinghe on 14 August 1918, his burial here is unusual as all the other Poperinghe executees (apart from one) are buried in Poperinghe New Military Cemetery.

4 Chaplains are buried here: The Reverend Charles I. S. Hood, attached 41st Royal Garrison Artillery, died on 15 April 1918, aged 31; The Reverend Cecil H. Schooling, attached 21st Infantry Brigade, died on 21 June 1917, aged 32; The Reverend R. W. Hopkins, Chaplain 4th Class, died on 24 April 1920 and The Reverend Charles E. Doudney, dubbed "the Beloved Chaplain Doudney" by his successor Philip Clayton, died aged 44, on 16 October 1915. On the 13th, with his next day's leave papers in his pocket, Doudney set out for one last visit to the front line at Potijze where, whilst assisting with a burial party, he was mortally wounded by shrapnel. Canon F. B. McNutt, who ministered to him during his last hours, later wrote:

Count him not dead, nor quenched the fiery spark of the Spirit which thus with duty kept its tryst. The swift shell struck - the pang - the mist - the dark! And then the Face of Christ.

The only woman buried here, one of two to die in the Salient, is 26-year old Staff Nurse Nellie Spindler, Queen Alexandra's Imperial Medical Nursing Service. She was killed on 21 August 1917, whilst attached to No. 44 Casualty Clearing Station at Brandhoek. Its War Diary records:

Yesterday morning the enemy began to shell the railway alongside the camp and the third or fourth shell killed S/Nurse Spindler. She was hit in the chest and died in about five minutes.' Four other nurses were concussed by the blast and the following day 44 Casualty Clearing Station, having evacuated all its nurses to St Omer, transferred to Remy Sidings where the officers and staff of 44 held a burial service for Staff Nurse Spindler.

Major Frederick Harold Tubb, V.C., Australian Infantry Force, who died on 20 September 1917, was awarded his Victoria Cross at Gallipoli in August 1915. In 1917 a newspaper reported:

Major Frederick Harold Tubb, VC., Australian Infantry, whose death from wounds is officially announced today, won the Victoria Cross at Lone Pine trenches in Gallipoli on 8 August. 1915. He then held the rank of Lieutenant. He was mortally wounded during the fighting on the Ypres front on Saturday. The gallant officer had been wounded, and was being carried back on a stretcher when he was struck by a shell.

Lieutenant-Colonel George E. Beatty-Pownall, D.S.O., 2nd Border Regiment, was the last British officer to be killed in the Salient. He died of wounds on 10 October 1918, aged 41, while commanding the 1st Battalion King's Own Scottish Borderers.

Captain Harold A. Chisenhale-Marsh, an Old Etonian and Staff Officer attached to 34th Division he died of wounds received near Kemmel on 28 September 1918. He joined the 9th Lancers in 1914, serving with them in the charge at Landrecies. The highest ranking officer to die in the Salient, Major-General M.S. Mercer, C.B., Officer Commanding 3rd Canadian Division, was killed on 3 June 1916, whilst he was making a routine inspection of the trenches near Armagh Wood during the Battle of Mount Sorrel. His body, recovered three weeks later, when the Canadians regained their lost positions, was brought back to Lijssenthoek for burial.

Row D Plots VII and VIII contain 93 burials of men of the British 4th and 29th Divisions who died in that counter-attack between 8–11 August.

The cemetery contains 7,350 British, 1,131 Australian, 1,053 Canadian, 658 French, 291 New Zealand, 32 Chinese, 29, South African, 21 British West Indies, 5 New Foundland, 3 American, 2 Indian, 1 Imperial War Graves Commission, 3 Known Unto God, and 223 German burials.

Abeele Aerodrome Cemetery is one of the few in this part of the salient designed by assistant to the principal architects, Major G. H. Goldsmith, most of his work being in the Ploegsteert area. Although named after it, this cemetery has no connection with the airfield that was sited nearby. The first burials here, 99 French soldiers and 4 British officers killed during the April

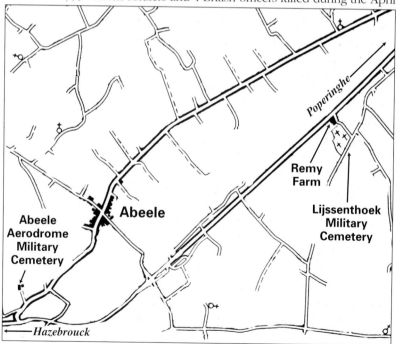

1918 German spring offensive, were added-to between July and September by a further 75 British and 84 American dead. After the Armistice the French and American dead were removed whilst 25 British soldiers, previously buried in Boeschepe Churchyard, were reburied here. The ground used for the removed French graves was utilised for these 25. The open space in front of the Great Cross was previously taken up with the American burials These were 84 men of the American 27th (New York) Division, attached to the British Second Army, who lost their lives in the fighting at Vierstraat on 1 September 1918. They had been stationed at Douglas Camp, Abeele, hence the choice of cemetery for their burials.

Approximate site of Abeele Aerodrome Military Cemetery which was first used as a burial plot in 1918

Bird's eye view of Abeele Airfield in 1915

The open space in front of the Great Cross was previously taken up with burials of men of the American 27th (New York) Division

Market day in the town square between the wars

10

POPERINGHE – A REMINDER

P OPERINGHE, unlike many of the towns and villages within the old
Ypres Salient, is much the same as it was in the war years. The town
centre has changed little, and most of the buildings that the officers
and men knew as cafés, estaminets, restaurants and theatres, are still in
place, with many housing the same, or a similar sort of business as they did
then. The two Switch Roads built by the British Army are still in use, serving
the same purpose they were designed for. Friday is still market day, and if
the town square was as much a hive of activity on Friday's then as it is now,
then no wonder the German airforce thought it a good time to run regular
bombing sorties. The embankment supporting the railway line that passed
through the centre of the town is still there in parts, and easily traceable in
others. The hospitals are marked by the cemeteries opened alongside them
in and around the town, and Talbot House is still operating in pretty much
the same way as it did during those years – the in-flow of soldiers replaced
by school parties and frequent visitors, some of whom choose to stay here
as a base for their visits to the old battlefields. The welcome is much the
same though, and everyone can be sure of the offer of a cup of tea the
minute they pass through its massive doors.

The sprawling suburbia of tin huts and 'shanties' have disappeared, now
replaced by a modern one of new houses, and an ever increasing complex
of business premises. The outlying farms are industrious and modernised –
the troops would no longer frown at the smells from cess- and slurry-pits,
or concern themselves with flies, lice and rats – and it does not take much
imagination to conjure up pictures of the many camps, dumps and Casualty
Clearing Stations that were sited in the surrounding fields.

What, most of all, Poperinghe has over other towns and villages in the
Salient, is a large number of descendants of its war time inhabitants. They
are knowledgeable of what happened here, and have memories of stories
their parents and grandparents told them. They care about their town and
its war-time history and are proud of it – and so they should be.

Talbot House at No. 35 Gasthuisstraat, apart from the flag poles, remains exactly as it was

No. 57 Gasthuisstraat, once *Skindles Hotel*, better known as the Officers' Club

A La Fabrique, retaining its original facade and the Flemish version of its name today – 't Fabriekje'

151

De Ranke, the old *La Poupée*, or Ginger's place as it was better known

L'Espérance, or 'What Hope', where Henry Williamson and 'Four toes' were 'ripped-off'

Den Nieuwen Haene, once *In den Ouden Haan* or, for the French, *Au Coq*

In de Vier Gekroonden, now the Hotel De Kring, which housed the Officer's Hostel

Today's war memorial stands where once stood the estaminet, *A la Maison de Ville*

De Hopbeurs and Du Tram, once the estaminets *A St Laurent* and *A La Fontaine* respectively, were both very popular with NCOs and other ranks

The houses, destroyed by the bomb that caused the church a 'near miss', were never rebuilt

In the town square, *The Coliseum* cinema (top), today's Belfort Hotel and, in Ieperstraat, *The Palace* cinema, today's Palace Hotel

2nd City of London Regiment (Royal Fusiliers) in the Great War (1914-1918). Major W. E. Grey, The Headquarters of the Regiment, 1929.

A Guide to the Western Front. Victor Neuberg, Penguin, 1988.

A Medico's Luck in the War. Colonel Rorie, D.S.O., T.D., M.D., D.P.H., Milne & Hutchison, 1929.

A Pilgrims Guide to the Ypres Salient. Toc H/Herbert Reiach, 1920.

A Subaltern's War. Charles Edmonds, Peter Davies Ltd., 1929.

A Surgeon in Khaki. Arthur Anderson Martin, M.D., Ch.B., F.R.C.S.E.D., Edward Arnold, 1915.

A Walk Round Plugstreet. Tony Spagnoly & Ted Smith, Leo Cooper, 1997.

Adventures of a Despatch Rider. Captain W. H. L. Watson. Dodd, Mead & Co.,1916.

British Regiments 1914-1918. Brig. E.A. James, Naval & Military Press, 1993.

Chavasse, Double VC. Ann Clayton, Leo Cooper, 1992.

Courage Remembered. G. Kingsley Ward & Major Edwin Gibson,HMSO, 1995.

Death's Men. Denis Winter, Allen Lane, 1978.

De Oorlog Achter Het Front. W. Tillie, C. Depoorter, S. Cossey, Poperinghe, 1987.

Eyewitness Accounts of the Great War. IFF, West Flanders, 1998.

Footprints of the 1/4th Leicestershire Regiment, August 1914 to November 1918. John Milne, Edgar Backus, 1935.

Fifty Amazing Stories of the Great War. Odhams, 1936.

From a Surgeon's Journal. 1915-1918. Harvey Cushing, Constable, 1936.

In Flanders Fields. Leon Wolff, Longman Green, 1959.

London Gunners. W. R. Kingham, M.A., Methuen & Co. Ltd., 1919.

Major & Mrs Holt's Battlefield Guide:Ypres Salient. Leo Cooper, 1997.

Martin-Leake, Double VC. Ann Clayton, Leo Cooper, 1994.

1914-1918,Voices and Images of the Great War. Lyn Macdonald, Michael Joseph, 1988.

Old Soldiers Never Die. Frank Richards, Faber & Faber, 1933.

Over There.A little guide for Pilgrims. Barclay Baron, Toc H, 1935.

Oxford Concise Companion to English Literature. Margaret Drabble & Jenny Stringer, Oxford University Press, 1996.

Plain Tales from Flanders. P.B. Clayton, Longman Green, 1930.

Rage of Battle. T. S. Hope, Tandem, 1965.

Salient Points One. Tony Spagnoly and Ted Smith. Pen & Sword, 1995.

Shell Shock. Anthony Babington, Leo Cooper, 1997.

Some Desperate Glory. E. Campion-Vaughan, Warne, 1981.

Talbot House, De Eerste Halte Na De Hel. J & K Louagie-Nolf, 1998.

Tales of Talbot House. P. B. Clayton, Geo Marshall & Co., 1928.

Undertones of War. Edmund Blunden, Cobden Sanderson, 1928.

Van Alle Markten Thuis. W. Tillie, Poperinghe, 1988.

Vignettes of the Western Front. Henry Lawson - Positif, 1979.

Walking the Salient. Paul Reed, Leo Cooper, 1999.

The 47th (London) Division, 1914-1918. Edited by Alan H. Maude, Amalgamated Press, 1922.

The Battle Book of Ypres. Beatrix Brice, John Murray, 1927.

The best of Fragments from France. Tonie & Valmai Holt, Milestone, 1978.

The Best of Good Fellows. Jonathan Horne, Jonathan Horne Publications, 1995.

The Bells of Hell Go Ting-A-Ling-A-Ling. Eric Hiscock, Arlington, 1976.

The. Cross of Sacrifice. Volume I. S. D. & D. B. Jarvis, 1993.

The Great War as I saw it. Canon Scott, Clarke & Stuart, 1934.

The Great War, I was there. Hammerton, 1938.

The History of the 12th (Bermondsey) Battalion East Surrey Regiment.
John Aston M.A. and L. M. Duggan, The Union Press, 1936.

The History of the Welsh Guards. C. H. Dudley Ward, D.S.O., M.C.
John Murry, 1920.

The Immortal Salient. Lieut.-Gen. Sir William Pulteney & Beatrix Brice, J. Murray,
1925.

The Imperial War Museum book of the Western Front. Malcolm Brown, BCA, 1993.

The Roses of No Man's Land. Lyn Macdonald, Papermac, 1984.

The Unending Vigil. Philip Longworth, Leo Cooper/Secker & Warburg, 1967.

The Victoria Cross, 1856-1920. J. B. Hayward, 1985.

The War Diary of the Master of Belhaven, 1914-1918. Lieut.-Col. the Hon. Ralph
Gerard Alexander Hamilton. D.S.O., M.D., Croix de Geurre avec palme,
John Murray, 1924.

The War the Infantry knew. Capt. J. C. Dunn, Cardinal, 1989.

The Wet Flanders Plain. Henry Williamson, The Beaumont Press, 1929.

The Wipers Times and after. Herbert Jenkins, London, 1918.

The Ypres Salient. Michael Scott, Gliddon Books, 1992.

With the First Canadian Contingent. Canadian Field Comforts Association, Hodder
& Stoughton, 1915.

World War 1914-1918, A Pictured History. Sir John Hammerton, The
Amalgamated Press, 1934.

Ypres and The Battles of Ypres. Michelin & Cie., 1919.

Private Papers - Paul Chapman.

Private Papers - Jaques Ryckebosch.

Private Papers - Ted Smith.

INDEX

POPERINGHE Streets, houses, hotels, restaurants, estaminets, cafés, theatres, shops and churches.

UNITS

1st Anzac Corps, No.29 Mobile Workshop –18
1st Battalion Inniskilling Fusiliers –11
1st Battalion King's Own Scottish Borderers –144
1st Battalion Welsh Guards –23, 99
1st Canadian Division –138
1st Life Guards –5
1st/5th Royal Warwickshire Regiment –31
1/8th Royal Warwickshire Regiment –11
2nd Battalion Duke of Wellington's Regt. –140
2nd Battalion Royal Welch Fusiliers, –9
2nd Cavalry Division –2
2nd City of Edinburgh Brigade –106
2nd Guards Brigade –17
2nd Leinster Regiment –48
2nd/5th Gloucestershire Regt. –109
3rd Canadian Division –145
4th Leicesters –24
5th Division –139
6th Battery Royal Field Artillery –128
6th London Regiment's Scottish Camp –93
7th London Regiment's Dominion Camp –93
9th Bat. Army Cyclist Corps –18
9th Bat. Lancashire Fusiliers –127
9th Bat. Royal Irish Fusiliers –131
9th Bat. South Staffs Regt. –121
12th (Bermondsey) East Surrey Regiment –53
12th Battalion Rifle Brigade –21
12th Battalion The Rifle Brigade –52, 56
13th Infantry Brigade –138
15th Division –84
19th Squadron Nieuport Scouts –113
148th Brigade, 49th West Riding Division. –114
27th (New York) Division –124, 146-147
30th (Tennessee) Division –124
33rd Battalion Machine Gun Corps –100
39th Divisional Field Ambulances –10
40th Pathans –139
47th (London) Division –102
47th Sikhs –139
55th (West Lancashire) Division –48, 86
71st Squadron Camel Scouts –113
87th and 89th French Territorial Division –3
Army Service Corps –20, 108-109
Border Regiment, –144
British Expeditionary Force –9
British West Indies Regiment –106
Canadian 3rd Division –139
Canadian Expeditionary Force –93
Chinese Labour Corps –119, 143
Chinese Labour Corps. –43
Chinese Labour Gangs –20, 109
Coldstream Guards –51
Durham Light Infantry –69
Fifth Army –113

German 36th Division (Uhlans) –2
German 3rd Cavalry Brigade –2
German 4th Cavalry –2
German High Command –1
Honourable Artillery Company –16
King's Own Scottish Borderers, –119
Lahore Division –138, 139
Light Railway Operating Coys. –133
Manchester Regiment, –21
Queen's Westminster Rifles –117
Tank Corps –125
Rifle Brigade –43
R.A. M.C. –10, 57, 60, 86, 78-79, 109
Royal Engineers –18, 20, 27
Royal Field Artillery –38
Royal Regiment –47
Royal Sussex Regiment –12
Royal Welch Fusiliers –41, 103
Second Army –124, 146
Scots Guards –90
The Welsh Guards –74
V Corps, 6th Division –4, 66
West Indian Labour Corps –106

BOOK TITLES

A Medico's Luck in the Great War –106
A Subaltern's War –31
A Surgeon in Khaki –96
A Trooper in the Tins –5
Adventures of a Despatch Rider –10
Air Command –138
Death's Men –35
Deeds That Thrill The Empire –139
Field Guns in France –47
Fireater –20
Footprints of the 1/4th Leicestershire Regiment –8
Stand To, A Diary of the Trenches –114
London Gunners –16
Lord Edward –11
Nomad Under Arms –44
Old Soldiers Never Die –9, 55
The War Diaries of The Master of Belhaven –97
The Great War as I saw it –25
The Wet Flanders Plain –39, 71
via Ypres –10

CAMPS

A.30 Central –110
A.30 Wood –99
Auckland –93
Boone Camp –100, 101
Browne Nos. 1, 2, and 3 –81, 109
Burgomaster Farm, Dickebusch West and New
Dickebusch –105
Canada Farm –137

Dirty Bucket Camp –74, 125, 110
Douglas Camp –146
Downshire Lines –103
Downshire Camp –93, 105
Dickebusch Huts –105
Micmac, Surrey and Warburg –105
Ontario, Quebec and Ottawa –93
Oakhanger and Ryde, –109
Peerless, North and South Atlantic, Zealand, Waratah, Moonta, Scrabo, Mud Farm –93
Pacific –93
Privet Camp –90
Red Horse Shoe –93
Siege Camp –74
Toronto, St. Lawrence, Erie, Winnipeg, Montreal, Halifax, Vancouver and Moose Jaw –93
Wellington –93

CEMETERIES

Brandhoek Military Cemetery –128
Brandhoek New Military Cemetery –128
Dozinghem Military Cemetery –135-136
Grootebeek British Cemetery –138
Gwalia Cemetery –125
Haringhe (Bandaghem) British Cemetery –133-134
Hospital Farm Cemetery –111
In Flanders Fields Cemetery, Waregem –143
Lijssenthoek Military Cemetery –121, 141
Mendinghem British Cemetery –131-132
Nine Elms British Cemetery –124
Poperinghe Communal Cemetery –117
Poperinghe New Military Cemetery –117, 144
Poperinghe Old Military Cemetery –65, 117
Reninghelst Churchyard and Extension Cemetery –139
Reninghelst New Military Cemetery –139
Tyne Cot Cemetery –141
Vlamertinghe Churchyard –139

CONCERT PARTIES

The Balmorals – 51st (Highland) Division, –48-49
The Crumps – 41st Division –48, 53
The Eighty Eights, The Whizzbangs and *The Duds* – Field Artillery. –48
The Fancies – 6th Division –48, 51-52, 100
The Follies – 4th Division –48-49
The Jocks – 15th Division –52
The Red Roses – 55th (West Lancashire) Division –48
The Roosters – 60th Division –48, 50
The Shrapnels – 33rd Division –48
The Smart Set – 4th Australian Division –48
The Tsjings – Chinese Labour Corps –48
The VA Dears – l'Hôpital Elizabeth –48

HOSPITALS/CASUALTY CLEARING STATIONS/ FIELD AMBULANCE

Bandagehem –91
Brandhoek Field Hospital –83
British Field Hospitals –87
CCS No. 3 Australian –83-84, 87
CCS Nos. 4, 12, 47, 61 –88
CCS Nos. 10 & 17 –87
CCS Nos. 32 –83
CCS No. 44 –144
CCS No. 46 –88, 90, 131
CCS Nos. 62 and 63 –88, 90
CCS No. 64 –88
CCS 3rd Canadian –87
Dozinghem –88, 135-136, 91
Field Ambulance –79, 83, 107
Field Ambulance No.15 –139
Field Ambulance No. 46 –84-85
Field Hospitals –83
French 15th Evacuation Hospital –87, 142
Gwalia Farm –56, 81, 106-107
Gwalia Farm Hospital –81, 125, 127
Hospital Elizabeth –78
l'Hôpital Elizabeth –48
Mendinghem –89, 90-91

A

Abeele –3, 18, 19, 66, 94, 100, 146
Abeele Aerodrome Cemetery –145
Abeele Airfield –146
Advanced Dressing Station –79-80, 128
Aid Post –129
Aid Station –118
Alexandra Farm –109
Area Provost Marshal –60-61, 75
Armagh Wood –145
Armentières –123
Armitage, Capt. Frank R. D.S.O., attd. 232rd Brigade Royal Field Artillery –130
Armstrong huts –20
Assher, Ben –44
Aston, Lieut. John –18, 25
Arthurs, Pte. –101

B

Bairnsfather –44
Baker, Pte. William, 26th Bat. Royal Fusiliers –143
Barker, Pte. R., L. 6th London Regt. –139
Baron Mazeman de Couthove –68, 77
Barrett, Cpl. Herbert, 2nd Btn. Worcestershire Regt. –117
Barry, Lieut.-Col. Frank D.S.O. –15
Batchelor, Major C.O., 'A' Battery, 59th Brigade –136